THINK
LIKE A
KING

NEIL SMITH

Cover design by Clara Yap.

Interior design by Timothy Chew.

Scripture quotations marked NLT are taken from the Holy Bible, New Living Translation. © 1996, 2004, 2007, 2013, 2015 by Tyndale House Foundation. Used by permission of Tyndale House Publishers, Inc., Carol Stream, Illinois 60188. All Rights Reserved.

Scripture quotations marked NIV are from the Holy Bible, New International Version, NIV, copyright © 1973, 1978, 1984, 2011 by Biblica, Inc. Used by permission of Zondervan. The "NIV" and "New International Version" are trademarks registered in the United States Patent and Trademark Office by Biblica, Inc.

Scripture quotations taken from the Amplified® Bible (AMP), Copyright © 2015 by The Lockman Foundation. Used by permission. www.Lockman.org"

Scripture quotations taken from the Amplified® Bible (AMPC), Copyright © 1954, 1958, 1962, 1964, 1965, 1987 by The Lockman Foundation Used by permission. www.Lockman.org

Scripture quotations are from the ESV® Bible (The Holy Bible, English Standard Version®), copyright © 2001 by Crossway, a publishing ministry of Good News Publishers. Used by permission. All rights reserved

Scripture quotations marked TPT are from The Passion Translation®. Copyright © 2017, 2018 by Passion & Fire Ministries, Inc. Used by permission. All rights reserved. ThePassionTranslation.com.

Scripture quotations marked NKJV are taken from the New King James Version®. Copyright © 1982 by Thomas Nelson. Used by permission. All rights reserved.

Scripture quotations marked MSG are taken from The Message, copyright © 1993, 2002, 2018 by Eugene H. Peterson. Used by permission of NavPress. All rights reserved. Represented by Tyndale House Publishers, Inc.

ISBN: 978-1-950247-07-3

Library of Congress Control Number: 2021931522

Before you dive in, scan here.

Throughout this book, you will see a few of these QR codes.

I encourage you to pause when you see them, scan the code and watch the video—don't skip it thinking that you will come back to it later! These are strategically placed in different chapters to correspond with what you are reading.

Some of these are testimonies and some are moments of prayer and impartation. They are designed to create room for God encounters as you read. I pray and believe that those moments will be what you remember most when you close this book and step into the fullness of your God-given purpose.

In addition to hearing from me, you'll also hear from other marketplace leaders and Kingdom influencers who have graciously contributed videos to this book.

Tim Costello

Glyn Barrett

Toure Roberts

Jiaheng & Adelene Chan

Melinda Munns

Kristine Brown

Craig Hughes

Their wisdom and experience is invaluable, and I know you will be inspired!

CONTENTS

ACKNOWLEDGEMENTS

This book is a summary of a lifetime of experiences, work and, most importantly to me, relationships.

I firstly thank Jesus for being my primary source of inspiration and unconditional love. You continue to astound me by choosing me (wow, why me??) to share this fresh revelation of how You have brought us into Your Kingdom and how we should think and live our lives as a result.

My father would have read this and relished in the fact that his years of gracious input, wise quotes and godly beliefs are in no small part embodied throughout this book. He would have read it and grabbed me by the arm, pulling me in closely and expressing how proud of me he was. Love you Dad. Miss you every day.

My mother's consistent, unwavering love and encouragement has built a foundation that has enabled me to have the courage to even dare to write this book.

My children—Kimberley, with her strength, determination and confidence, and Ryan, with his passion, drive and sense of humour—give me a constant sense of pride and satisfaction.

Russell and Sam, thank you for your leadership and friendship over the years. Because of your relentless faith and breakthrough belief, I dare to dream that this book will not only communicate information, but also create defining moments of encounter.

Thanks also to the team who worked on this book—Megan, Tim, Clayton—and extra thanks to my assistant Joey, without whom I would only have achieved a small percentage of the many major milestones God has enabled me to attain.

Finally, to my one and only favourite, Leonie—you have stood by my side for over 30 years, never giving up on me, stirring me to be the greatest I can be, so often deferring your dreams for mine and always pushing me to go higher. This book is 50% YOU. Like so many of the things we've achieved, it is OURS. For you, I am forever grateful.

I dedicate this book to you as a small token of my love and gratitude for the lifetime that you have stood by my side.

ENDORSEMENTS

Russell Evans
Senior Pastor, Planetshakers
Australia

Think Like A King accelerates within you exactly what it suggests. Our individual and collective experiences condition our thinking and ultimately either accelerate or destabilise our lives. In order to live out our God-given destinies, our thinking has to be in line with God's. A book such as this, necessitates that it is written by a practitioner and not just a theorist. I have known Neil Smith for nearly two decades. The material in this book has been tried, tested and proven time and again in nations all over the world and within my own personal setting in Europe. To *think like a king* necessitates both time with the King, and walking with kingly people. Neil is a King-maker and this book will enable you to think and lead in a manner that is truly transformational!

Glyn Barrett
Senior Pastor, !Audacious Church
National Leader, Assemblies of God in Great Britain
United Kingdom

In *Think Like A King*, Neil Smith challenges all of us to live with the mindset of royalty. This challenge to bring Kingdom principles to the marketplace is needed in every nation on Earth. Neil's experience with the Planetshakers global movement and national impact initiatives strategically positions him to lead God's people in bringing the King's influence to the world. Neil is a friend, a world-changer and one of the great strategic minds in the church today. You will be blessed by this book!

Dr William M. Wilson
President, Oral Roberts University
Chair, Pentecostal World Fellowship
Global Co-Chair, Empowered21
United States of America

At Boshoff
Global Founder, Christian Revival Church
South Africa

We have very influential businesspeople in our church that would love to preach from my platform. Unfortunately, they haven't understood that their own platform in the marketplace is just as important, because they are reaching people that might otherwise never come to church. Neil has been a blessing for our church because he's helped us to see things differently. This refreshing perspective is what gives him the authority to write about being a *light* in the marketplace.

Andrew Corson
Senior Pastor, Su Presencia
Colombia

When the young prophet Elisha emerged fresh out of the Jordan, carrying the double portion anointing he had just received from heaven, the first thing he did was to respond to the desperate cry of the city elders to come and heal a city that had become broken, bitter and unproductive. Elisha simply asked them for a bowl of salt and to be led to the wellspring of the city where the people drank. Pouring the bowl of salt into the wellspring, Elisha declared, "I have healed the waters of the city!"

Neil Smith is a modern-day Elisha—his message, his ministry and his relentless passion to see cities and nations transformed have all resulted in producing modern day miracles of healing and transformation in communities and cities around the world.

Every page of Neil's book *Think Like A King* is infused with faith, revelation, kingdom strategies, and supernatural motivation to call us from our encounter to our assignment, from our Jordan to the wellsprings of modern-day society. Whether you're a politician or a businessperson, a church leader or a young professional, let *Think Like A King* be a double portion mantle in your hand to empower you to bring influence to every area of your world!

Martin Steel
Global Team, Kingdomcity
New Zealand

Marcus Lamb
Founder and President, Daystar Television Network
United States of America

 WATCH VIDEO

Truly a great book on the topic of leadership and dominion! Neil Smith has clearly articulated the need for the church and the marketplace to be united to achieve the greater purpose of God. He has also given the necessary principles and steps to achieve this. The hand of God and the voice of the Holy Spirit are so obviously evident throughout this book. A must read for pastors and leaders!

Saras Bany
Senior Pastor, Audacity Malaysia
Malaysia

INTRODUCTION

Raised in the House

I will never take for granted the fact that I enjoyed an amazing, secure and loving home life as a child growing up. My parents, who immigrated to Australia from England when I was 6 months old, loved each other, loved their family and worked hard to build a brand new life—oceans away from all that was familiar to them. They faced significant personal losses and took on great risk to give my siblings and I the best opportunity to be happy and successful in every way possible.

Mum and Dad were always fully committed to their local church which became the hub around which our schedules revolved. Every Sunday began early with Sunday School for kids, followed by a morning service. After the service, we would head home for lunch. Those were the days when it was considered 'worldly' to go to the shops on the Sabbath, but Mum and Dad were always a little more flexible with these religious 'rules' than the other parents and would regularly sneak into the local fish and chip shop for a quick lunch. Often we would bump into fellow church-goers hoping not to be seen and Dad would just smile and nod as if to silently agree never to speak of the encounter again.

After lunch, we would drive to another location to help with the children's ministry of a new church plant before heading back to our own church for the evening service which would run well into the night. In addition to Sunday services, we were wholeheartedly committed to weekly small groups, mid-week night meetings, youth services, camps and all kinds of social functions like church picnics, outreaches, Busy Bee clean-ups and visits to the sick and elderly. Our life literally revolved around the local church and we loved it. Some of my greatest memories today are of the adventures I experienced and the friendships I made during those childhood years.

For my family, church was not negotiable. Nothing was more important than attending church and there was no excuse—short of hospitalisation or death—that would be deemed valid enough for staying at home. Attending and actively serving in our local church was entrenched in me from childhood and something that I have since entrenched in the lives of my own children. This unmoving, non-negotiable boundary line that was set into the foundations of my life by my parents is one of the things that I will always be most grateful for, as it has enabled me and my own family to flourish beyond anything I could have imagined.

> **Attending and actively serving in our local church was entrenched in me from childhood and something that I have since entrenched in the lives of my own children.**

> *Those who are planted in the house of the Lord shall flourish in the courts of our God.*
>   *— Psalm 92:13 (NKJV)*

From my earliest memories, I recall my dad serving on the church board, overseeing the business and financial affairs of the church for many years of his life. Over the decades that we consistently attended the same church, we saw several senior pastors come and go, but regardless of who was at the helm at any given time, my dad remained faithful in serving—season in and season out.

My father worked loyally for the same company for 36 years as the Australian Regional Operations Manager for A.C. Nielson's Market Research, before retiring. His broad experience equipped him to speak into the financial and business affairs of the church, but he was also a very social man who loved people and used every opportunity to speak into their lives and help them in whatever ways he could. People loved him, though it wasn't until his funeral that I came to realise just how much. He had a special blend of ministry and business gifting which was difficult for people to understand in those early days. Though fully committed to his local church, his job would often require him to travel and frequently miss church events which would make him unpopular with leaders who would sometimes label him 'unspiritual'. However, despite his absences from church, he always ensured that his house and car were available for ministry when needed, and that his giving was generous and consistent—especially when called on to support special projects and outreaches.

I only remember pastors visiting my dad when finance was needed. He never complained about this, but now, having spoken with many business people over the years who have had similar experiences, I know it must have been difficult to reconcile. Yet like no one else I have ever known, he kept his heart pure and continued to respond faithfully to each need that presented itself. It was clear that he had been pigeon-holed as a businessman and moneymaker, apparently excluding him from opportunities to serve in more 'spiritual' ministry areas. These were the days of either/or, where a successful ministry path required a person to leave their career to take up paid ministry in a church. The idea of a businessperson finding ministry expression in addition to their job, was virtually unheard of. It was assumed that pastoring people AND working a job would leave a person torn between two incompatible worlds.

What I didn't know as a child growing up was that my dad was helping to forge a new path for a future reality in which ministry calling and marketplace career could coexist—even flourish.

An Emerging Call

From my earliest memories, I knew I was called to pastoral ministry. The conviction was strong, even as a young man, and never left me despite my occasional wanderings as a teenager and young adult when the world was bombarding me with attractive possibilities. As a child, I remember running church services in my bedroom, lining up teddy bears and setting up all of the equipment I needed (having attended and watched countless actual church services). With great passion I would welcome the bears, lead praise and worship using the overhead projector, then preach up a storm. Inevitably, all of those present would give their lives to Jesus and I would close the service feeling proud of myself. I was about 11 years old at the time.

Guest ministers attending our church would frequently prophesy over me to the dismay of my pastors who had to deal with my troublemaking long after they had left. The declaration over me was always the same—that I would speak before crowds of thousands, have great influence over youth for the Kingdom of God, travel extensively and be involved in significant church ministries and missions endeavours.

My parents never pressured me to pursue the ministry—quite the opposite in fact. My mum grew up in a ministry household that always struggled financially and she experienced first-hand the pressures that ministry life in the 1950's and 1960's placed on families in England. Her catchcry was, "Who would ever want to be in the ministry?" However, despite her strong feelings on the subject, she was always supportive of my decisions, making sure that I clearly understood that ministry was a calling and not a choice to be made lightly. I'm so grateful to her for her wisdom on this. Unlike some ministry parents who pressured their children to go into the ministry and only validated and accepted them when they did, or others who threatened to disown their children if they did not pursue a 'real' career in the 'real' world (outside the church walls), I didn't feel any such pressure and was free to pursue whatever God had placed in my heart to do.

I basically went on to fail my way through school. My brother and sister pursued well-paid careers, but school didn't work for me. As a result, I was a difficult student who frustrated my teachers and led other kids astray. My leadership gift was emerging in an immature form, but I wasn't using it for good, that's for sure.

My mum tells the story about the day she returned from one of many parent-teacher interviews where she was told, yet again, that I was out of control and destined to fail. She was understandably upset and began to pray about the situation. She felt the Lord say that the very behaviours and personality traits that I was manifesting and being criticised for were the very same things that He would use in my life in the years to come. All that He required her to do was to establish firm boundaries, consistently discipline me and love me unconditionally. She said that the burden of raising me lifted off her that same day and she set about obeying the instructions of the Lord. I'd like to say that I was a dream child, but what I can say is that she did something right. I went on to devote my life to serving Jesus, along with my household, and as a parent myself now, it doesn't get much better than that!

My dad refused to conform to the standard belief that there was only one path to a good career: School—University—Job. Instead, he challenged us to give our best effort to the tasks before us and follow wherever the path took us to find our purpose in life. Essentially, he was confirming the words of Psalm 37:

The steps of a good man are ordered by the Lord,
And He delights in his way.
Though he fall, he shall not be utterly cast down;
For the Lord upholds him with His hand.
— *Psalm 37:23-24 (NKJV)*

After showing some skill in a woodworking class, Dad suggested I try a carpentry apprenticeship. I am so thankful that he identified my potential instead of focusing on my shortcomings. I am of the belief that just as you can mistake the first shoots of a plant for weeds or common grass, the early evidence of our gifting can so easily be mistaken for unwanted traits. Fortunately, my dad recognised my leadership and entrepreneurial strengths, and encouraged me to develop them. At the same time, he did not hold back in applying consistent discipline. I will always be grateful for his releasing spirit and his wise counsel throughout my life.

After leaving school to study carpentry and joinery, I was offered a number of apprenticeships and accepted one with one of Australia's then best-known building companies—AV Jennings. I served that company for three years in their construction division, earning significantly more money than some of my more academic peers. However, the call of God remained strong and I continued to serve as Youth Pastor in my childhood church, in a volunteer capacity. This is where I found real joy and fulfilment, although I loved my carpentry job as well. It was the best of both worlds as I was able to serve in the ministry while at the same time, supporting myself and my young family.

In the final year of my apprenticeship, I sustained an ankle injury while playing basketball and was unable to work on the tools. My company had no choice but to relocate me to the site office for five months where I went on to flourish in site management and supervision. Once again, my leadership gift was emerging, maturing and finding expression in any environment I found myself in. During that time, I earned the trust of the company's executives and was given unusual access and insight into their private lives beyond the workplace. Knowing that I was a Christian Youth Pastor who personally chose not to drink alcohol, I was often the nominated driver for social functions which allowed me to interact with their family members and at times sit at tables and witness high level business transactions.

I really enjoyed this new role and learned so much that still assists me today in my various roles at Planetshakers Church and in other settings. The company recognised my gifting and instead of releasing me at the end of my apprenticeship, offered me a construction cadetship involving further building-related college study while concurrently working onsite in project management and as a site foreman. These were great days where God was adding layers of gifting and experience to my calling that would prove invaluable later in life. Not everything I witnessed was positive, helpful, legal or character building, but God taught me invaluable lessons during that season of my life.

Right at the moment when my building career was surging forward with new opportunities for advancement presenting daily, I was offered a paid position as Youth Pastor—the role I had been serving in as a volunteer for some time. Obviously, my manager was not the only one who recognised my growing leadership gift at the time. I was faced with a difficult choice as I loved my building career AND my ministry role.

Choosing to pursue ministry was never an escape for me. When I finally obeyed the prompting of the Holy Spirit and left the building industry, I really missed it. I missed the thrill of chasing down deals, connecting with high level business and government identities, wooing potential clients, and most of all, the material benefits. I was newly married and the financial security of my building career was very attractive. However, the deep satisfaction and joy of knowing that I was in the centre of God's will for my life more than made up for the losses I felt, and I embraced my ministry role wholeheartedly. Despite my love for the ministry, I did wrestle with the pull back to the business arena for years after the decision was made.

In 1997, my wife Leonie and I followed the call of God to plant a church and stepped into a whole new level of leadership responsibility. Realising that as the senior pastors, we had a responsibility to model our fledgling church's culture on the culture of Heaven, I set about seeking God to discover, in greater revelation, the core values of His Kingdom and His divine mandate for our church and the city that we loved.

From the very beginning, I knew I could never be content pastoring a small, suburban church—not that there's anything wrong with that. Working in industry had opened my eyes to the world beyond the walls of the church—a world that revolved around seizing and maintaining power and influence in a city. I had learned first-hand that whoever carried authority in a given arena had the power to set culture and determine the atmosphere under which the powerless had to live and work. I had learned that money changes everything and that whoever has it also has power and influence at tables where decisions are made. I had observed that our city had very clear supply lines that kept its cogs turning— education, health, business and church—and that whoever controlled these supply lines was empowered to set its culture and determine the long-term health and prosperity of all who lived within its borders. As I reflect on this, I realise that God was teaching me how to think *like a king*.

I could not shake the growing revelation that God's intention for His people was far broader than their salvation alone. He was deeply interested in their security, prosperity, justice, health, education and peace. Jesus had not only come to redeem the lost, but to usher in the Kingdom of

We were not just called to bide our time while awaiting Jesus' return, but to rule, reign and govern our world according to the original mandate spoken over mankind at creation. Heaven, and with it, 'life and life to the full'. We were not just called to bide our time while awaiting Jesus' return, but to rule, reign and govern our world according to the original mandate spoken over mankind at creation:

> *Then God blessed them and said, "Be fruitful and multiply. Fill the earth and govern it...*
> — *Genesis 1:28 (NLT)*

I began to see clearly that God never intended for His church to sit back and simply accept living within a culture shaped by the governance and decision-making of those who are not Kingdom-minded. Instead, He intended that His sons and daughters live with the revelation of their royal lineage, a clear understanding of their divine calling, an authentic and relentless love for people, and bold access to His anointing, empowerment and the resources of Heaven. He equipped us with intelligence, wisdom, skill and creativity to sit at the gateways of our city, guarding the supply lines and wielding influence that would facilitate the establishment of His Kingdom's culture and values in every sphere of society. God's intention was that His people, committed to excellence, would rule over their assigned realms, managing God-given resources and rising to places of influence where decisions are made and the consequences felt throughout a society. God desired to see His creation flourish in every area of their lives...and of course, that ALL would be saved.

> *For this is good and acceptable in the sight of God our Savior, who desires all men to be saved and to come to the knowledge of the truth.*
> — *1 Timothy 2:3-4 (NKJV)*

I came to realise that church is intended and called to be far more than an ark where deliverance from a fallen world can be found. It is instead called to be a place where kings and queens-in-waiting can be spiritually reborn, raised in the knowledge of God and called and equipped for Kingdom purpose. It is where grown kings can find refuge, encounter God and be refreshed, restored and empowered in readiness for their return to the realm over which they are called to rule. It is the place where kings and queens can seek wisdom to aid them in their rulership, strategize for kingdom expansion and direct the flow of resources for Kingdom exploits.

This was a very different vision to anything I had experienced in my life up until that point.

God had allowed me to see something that I could not unsee: a city desperately waiting for the royal sons and daughters of God to rise up, take their positions of authority and rule with godly principles that create Kingdom culture.

> *For the creation waits in eager expectation for the children of God to be revealed. For the creation was subjected to frustration, not by its own choice, but by the will of the one who subjected it, in hope that the creation itself will be liberated from its bondage to decay and brought into the freedom and glory of the children of God.*
>
> *— Romans 8:19-21 (NIV)*

It was then that a burden to win cities was deposited by God in my spirit and has never lifted since.

Cities to Be Won

Unfortunately, the church I had been raised in had modelled that most ministry happens within its sacred four walls—should people choose to come inside them. At best, Christians were encouraged to take the message of Christ out to the streets during official evangelistic outreaches, bearing some fruit but having little, if any, impact on their city at large. Though I would never underestimate the power of just one soul saved, I saw these events like striking a match in the middle of the night—a small flash of light that was virtually undetectable and temporary in impact.

There seemed to be a large, man-made divide between what went on in the Church and what went on in the marketplace (the realm of business, trade and economics). While this remained in place, the enemy seemed undaunted by the Church as long as she kept her distance from his territory, remained relatively unaware of her power and mandate, and only produced insignificant and short-lived flashes of light in the overwhelming darkness. In turn, the Church seemed content to operate within the confines of her walls—willing and available, but relatively contained and starved of the resources needed to fulfil her mandate.
This divide between the Church and the marketplace all too often meant that Christian businesspeople were left unequipped to bring Kingdom influence to the marketplace and live the life of dominion that God had purposed for them. My friendships with many Christians of influence showed me how common it was for believers to cave to the pressures of their environments and conform to the patterns of the world, rather than to think like kings and live out their God-given destinies. Many corporate executives and affluent entrepreneurs, Christian and non-Christian alike, attained success as defined by their bank balances and business shareholdings, but lost the things that truly mattered. Instead of being change agents, they assimilated into the prevailing marketplace culture.

The Church was falling short of its mandate to raise kings and queens who were ready to transform culture, change mindsets and win cities for the glory of God.

I couldn't be satisfied with this situation and began to dream of ways that the Gospel might infiltrate every level of society and begin to do its work in changing culture and lighting a fire that could not easily be ignored or quenched.

I began to see the latent potential of the Church to advance the Kingdom of God exponentially if we could just mobilise the vast majority of churchgoers who would NEVER be in a full-time church role but had access to places that the Church would never step into. I wondered what would happen if every Christian operated as a minister of the Gospel within their own unique sphere of influence and in every layer of society—education, health, business, arts, science, construction, politics etc.—using

I began to see the latent potential of the Church to advance the Kingdom of God exponentially.

their influence to establish Kingdom culture and Kingdom thinking within their assigned territory. I could see ordinary men and women of God sharing their faith, pointing out the way to the House of God and bringing the lost into its doors to find salvation, healing, belonging, destiny and family.

I knew what God had placed on my heart but it wasn't going to just happen overnight. It would require a significant mindset change for the Church at large in order to see that ministry was never intended to be limited to it's four walls, and in particular, to the pulpit—but that it could and should be conducted in every sphere of personal influence, including the marketplace. Marketplace ministry needed to become the 'new normal' of Christian living and church growth, with every Christian recognising and embracing their higher call:

> *But you are a chosen generation, a royal priesthood,*
> *a holy nation, His own special people, that you may*
> *proclaim the praises of Him who called you out of*
> *darkness into His marvelous light.*
>
> — *1 Peter 2:9 (NKJV)*

So to you who are reading this book today—thank you for coming on this journey. I want to encourage you from the outset to open your mind to new possibilities and embrace the challenge of the Apostle Paul to position yourself for transformation by intentionally renewing your mind.

> *Do not conform to the pattern of this world, but be*
> *transformed by the renewing of your mind. Then you will*
> *be able to test and approve what God's will is—his good,*
> *pleasing and perfect will.*
>
> — *Romans 12:2 (NIV)*

What if we are waiting for God to bring transformation to society while He is waiting for US to rise up in the authority He has called us to? What if our limited thinking is restricting the expansion of God's Kingdom in the kingdoms of the Earth? What if the change that you long to see in your workplace or your business actually depends on you getting a revelation that you are called to rule?

It's time to *think like a king*!

INTRODUCTION

WINNING CITIES

You are the light of the world. A city that is set on a hill cannot be hidden. Nor do they light a lamp and put it under a basket, but on a lampstand, and it gives light to all who are in the house. Let your light so shine before men, that they may see your good works and glorify your Father in heaven.

— Matthew 5:14-16 (NKJV) —

We are called to declare God's will and intention rather than be dictated to by prevailing mindsets and cultural norms.

"You are the light of the world"...such a simple statement, yet so packed with responsibility and privilege! God has called us to lead, not follow. We are called to rule as kings and queens, not be ruled. We are called to declare God's will and intention rather than be dictated to by prevailing mindsets and cultural norms. Scripture puts it this way:

> **And the LORD will make you the head and not the tail;**
> **you shall be above only, and not be beneath...**
> **— Deuteronomy 28:13 (NKJV)**

Jesus, in His sermon on the mount, used the metaphor of *light* to help the crowd understand their significance in activating His Kingdom on Earth. Notice here that there is no suggestion that functioning as spiritual light in darkness is optional for the Christian or only for those who officially work in ministry. Instead, He made the definitive declaration that we ARE the light of the world—light being part of our very nature and intrinsic to our being as followers of Jesus.

In those days, a typical lamp used in the home was a small vessel made of clay with a hole in the top for the oil and a spout to hold a wick which would be lit and would burn as long as there was enough oil to fuel it. Because the lamps were small, they were most effective when placed high on a lampstand to allow the flame to illuminate an entire room, allowing people to move around freely. When the sun rose, a bowl would be put over the lamp to limit the oxygen and extinguish the flame. We can see now why Jesus was the master of using everyday concepts to illustrate spiritual principles!

Called to Shine

In calling us *light*, Jesus was describing our call to illuminate the Kingdom of God in the darkness of our fallen world. Our lives are to be an ongoing testimony of the reality of Christ's Presence and power at work. It is the light of His Presence in us that we are to steward carefully and allow to shine without hindrance. We may feel like our flame is small and insignificant, but even the smallest flame can be positioned for great influence. When many small flames are brought together, the combined light suddenly reaches a point of saturation and significance, not only illuminating the space immediately around it, but also becoming visible from a distance!

Note also that Jesus specifically said that such a light CANNOT be hidden. This is best illustrated when you try to get away to the country for a break and realise that although you have travelled a significant distance, there is a glow on the horizon that reminds you that you live in a city that creates a huge amount of light from many small sources. Clearly, there comes a point when no amount of 'bowls' can extinguish the accumulated light, reminding us that there is incredible power to be found in joining together as the Body of Christ—with unity of mind and purpose!

I am reminded of a story from my childhood that illustrates this principle well. In 1962, John Glenn became the first American to orbit the Earth in the Friendship 7 spacecraft. On this mission, Glenn flew over Perth, Western Australia, and the people of Perth, feeling great empathy for the isolated, lone astronaut, turned on their lights to acknowledge his mission. Glenn observed that the city was clearly visible from space and Perth became known worldwide as the 'City of Light'. This was repeated in 1998 and I was able to be a part of it. Leading up to the 50th anniversary of the 1962 event, John Glenn thanked the many thousands of people who turned their lights on and rushed out into their backyards to wave torches towards the night sky. He said he could still recall the moment he saw Perth light up below him as he passed over the city in the Friendship 7 spacecraft. "It just seems like it was yesterday to me", he said, "I remember that view very vividly."

Because thousands of people chose to switch on their lights in unison that night against the backdrop of thick darkness, the scope of the light produced reached far beyond what any individual light could have. The piercing light, clearly visible from space, not only captivated and impacted the space traveller personally, but also put an otherwise insignificant city on the world map and in the world's news headlines!

Light speaks to me of influence, something business people often neglect in their pursuit of finance. Money is important. Without it, very little can be accomplished. But influence—now that is something that is truly powerful, difficult to contain and impossible to measure!

Jesus Himself is the greatest example of this. He did not need riches in order to exert influence. He simply allowed His Kingdom to be seen and demonstrated through His life daily, providing a stark contrast to the world around Him. Wherever He went, He left an indelible impression on those who encountered Him. He was regularly found in spiritually *dark* places. Consider His meal at the tax collector's house, His conversation with a broken woman at the well and His interruption of the stoning of the woman found in adultery. In each of these scenarios, not only did He show up where He was least expected to be (as a 'man of the cloth'—so to speak), but He also radically transformed the lives of every individual who came into contact with Him and the countless others who gathered around to watch Him shine from a distance. Like moths to a streetlight, people were drawn irresistibly to the light that came from inside of Him.

Imagine if He had chosen instead to base Himself in the temple each day, preaching with passion and urging people to come in, but never taking His message to the streets and marketplaces where the people were going about their daily lives. Would His influence have spread so rapidly that He was able to change the course of history in just three years?

So it should be in our everyday lives. Whether in ministry, business or any other field of endeavour, we should have a powerful effect on others, drawing them to the light in us and pointing them to the reality of Jesus Christ. This is the calling of EVERY believer and as such, we are ALL called to be ministers of the Gospel, regardless of our vocation. Collectively, we have an even higher calling—to win cities and reform culture by using our influence to see the Kingdom of God made manifest on Earth.

While the mandate and message are the same for us all, the *forum* or *arena* in which we declare or reveal that message is highly dependent on our unique God-given calling. While for some, it is the pulpit; for others, it is the marketplace. Jesus was intimately familiar with and completely comfortable in both settings! Having said that, He did not always allow His light to shine brightly out in the open. Yes, there were many times when He stood before crowds and very publicly declared the truth of His Kingdom. However, there were also times when He remained silent or quietly slipped through the crowd and withdrew, deliberately containing His light so that it could only be seen by a chosen few.

We learn from Jesus that in all of our shining, there is a time to be *overt* and a time to be *covert*. Though the light does not stop shining, it can be targeted and focussed to achieve a particular, effective outcome. The same is true with our faith. Wisdom should never be far away as we display the Kingdom of God in our daily lives.

Set Apart

To *shine* is our primary calling as Christians, no matter what our occupation. Why? Matthew 5:16 tells us clearly—to *glorify* the Father. According to Strong's Concordance, the word 'glorify' is translated from the Greek word *doxazo*. This word is used to mean "to cause the dignity and worth of a person or thing to become manifest and acknowledged", and to "praise enthusiastically (extol), magnify, celebrate, honour, make renown and render as excellent". Wow. I'm not sure about you, but Jesus' words now seem so much weightier. What a privilege and awesome responsibility we have in being able to affect the reputation of God on Earth by what we do or fail to do. And what powerful motivation to praise, celebrate and honour Him!

So if it is the job of every Christian to shine in the darkness and make the Father famous, why does the Church at large still not occupy the highest position of influence on the earth? Surely this is our mandate? Perhaps we have underestimated the fact that true influence comes through excellence and integrity—both of which we can so frequently neglect as we are swallowed up in the culture of the corporate world in which we work. In conforming to the culture of the marketplace, we lose our point of difference and fail to draw any attention to ourselves and to the God we represent. But Scripture makes it clear we are not called to *conform*, but rather to be *transformed*:

> *I beseech you therefore, brethren, by the mercies of God, that you present your bodies a living sacrifice, holy, acceptable to God, which is your reasonable service. And do not be conformed to this world, but be transformed by the renewing of your mind, that you may prove what is that good and acceptable and perfect will of God.*
> *— Romans 12:1-2 (NKJV)*

Souls and Cities

As a young boy growing up in a Pentecostal church, I clearly remember what *missions* looked like. Usually it would involve sending teams of adventurous, well-intentioned volunteers to another country for a few days to support a missionary on the ground or serve in an orphanage or small church setting. We would send some food or other needed items that would bring temporary relief—mostly items from our own cupboards that we didn't want or were out of date. It's quite shameful now, thinking back on the mindset that missionaries should be 'blessed' with the leftovers and unwanted items of those who lived in relative affluence. Undoubtedly, the missionaries would be encouraged and people would come to salvation, but just as quickly as teams arrived, they would leave to return home with a great story of their adventures in a foreign land but leaving very little lasting change behind them. Was anything of real significance established as a result of our efforts? Sadly, not really.

I have been privileged to get up close and personal with some of the greatest evangelists of my lifetime. Reinhard Bonnke was one of my heroes. In his lifetime, he saw 79 million recorded decisions for Christ in crusades all around the world. Absolutely incredible! But when you go to some of those countries today, you find them in the same condition, if not worse, than they were in when they experienced radical revival through these great men and women of God. Without doubt, countless lives were transformed and many saved from an eternity without God, but very little systemic change could be felt in their nation in the weeks, months and years after the evangelists had packed up their tents and moved on.

Something was missing. Could it be that evangelism alone is not enough to see permanent transformation of a city and its culture?

My parents-in-law were missionaries in Papua New Guinea during a time when travel, technology and communication were greatly inferior to what they are today. I am so grateful for the part they played in preparing the way for the missions work I am involved with today and would never intentionally underestimate the fruit of their labour in introducing Christianity to a nation steeped in spiritual darkness. However, with the tools and technology we have today, there is no excuse to settle for the level of influence and impact experienced by previous generations. So why do we still remain relatively ineffective at establishing long-term change that accurately reflects the redemptive power of the Gospel?

I believe that the answer lies in our *thinking*.

We are living in an era where transformational thinking is absolutely critical. It isn't enough to accept 'pebble in a stream' impact when God has called and equipped us to exert 'earthquake-level', 'nation-shaping' impact. The Church today has the ability to reach beyond its walls to not only impact its local population, its city and its nation, but all the nations of the Earth!

> **Ask of Me, and I will give You**
> **The nations for Your inheritance,**
> **And the ends of the earth for Your possession.**
> — *Psalm 2:8 (NKJV)*

There has never been such great opportunity to influence the world for the glory of God, so what is the blockage? Why are we not seeing whole nations come to Jesus? The simple answer is that if it's not happening, something needs to change, and change of any kind begins in our *thinking*.

The dilemma of a lack of lasting change following significant missions endeavours was the catalyst for me to examine my own thinking. Faced with

SCAN & WATCH

a mandate from my senior pastor to "look into how we can invest into neighbouring nations" (having freely received and wanting to freely give—as per Jesus' commandment in Matthew 10:8), I began to ask myself the question, How can we really bring systemic change to Papua New Guinea? Whereas in the past I might have called in a group of pastors and spiritual leaders to discuss the matter, this time I felt to gather business people who were experts in their field and ask them the same question. After three days of deliberation, I was left with one simple directive to write to the nation's leader and request a meeting. So I did.

I had no idea what I might say to this man if he should respond, and partly hoped he wouldn't. I had no '10-point plan' or great sales pitch, just a mandate from God to make a start and obey step 1. To my surprise, the Prime Minister of the nation responded to my letter, expressing that he would meet me to discuss the needs of his nation. It was on. I had no idea what I was going to say and collapsed on my pillow that night, stressed out. I should have known better. God woke me in the middle of the night and began to download a strategy for bringing systemic change to the nation of Papua New Guinea. In short, He spoke to me about 5 specific areas of change:

1. *Leadership*—speaking into people's mindsets
2. *Commerce*—raising hope for the future through opportunity
3. *Education*—building capacity in people
4. *Health*—optimising each person's ability to thrive and contribute
5. *Church*—awakening the nation spiritually to the Kingdom of God.

This encounter with God deeply impacted me and I wrote down everything He spoke in detail so that I could present it to the Prime Minister. Most interesting was the fact that church was last on the list, which seemed to contradict my entire belief system. But the more I thought about it, the more I began to realise that even when people have a life-changing salvation encounter with God, they will inevitably fail to thrive spiritually if they continue to struggle with hunger, sickness, lack of resources and education, and feelings of hopelessness and despair. God is a holistic God who cares deeply about the welfare of His children, and His vision for Kingdom-impact on Earth may well be far broader than we have traditionally defined it.

By seeking to influence a nation's leadership, commerce, education, health and church structures, we can begin to understand the natural and spiritual powers at play and find ways of working with them to bring sustainable change and in the process, see the Kingdom of God advance. Ultimately, God is glorified and churches begin to function in the power of their calling. Seeking salvation is the natural response when people realise that the silent cries of their heart are being heard as they watch the challenging conditions of their everyday lives radically and miraculously turn around!

When I finally sat down with the Prime Minister of Papua New Guinea and presented the 5 focus points for systemic change, the real journey began. Doors began to fly open, resources were offered to me and like-minded business people, professionals and ministries gathered to the vision to engage in this nation-building endeavour. Since then, and having seen the results in neighbouring countries, other leaders have pursued me for guidance and urged me to replicate the process in their nations.

I don't tell this story to brag. The continued success of the *Believe* campaigns in the South Pacific nations has had nothing to do with me. God was simply looking for someone to think differently—to open their mind to new perspectives and new ways of approaching old problems. I am humbled and grateful that He chose me to be a conduit of this change, but it all began when I looked for a Kingdom-solution to a natural problem. What I didn't realise was that I was positioning my seemingly insignificant *light* in the hand of God, to be elevated to a place where it could be seen and draw others with their own lights. Together, we are beginning to shine brightly, attracting global attention, making a significant impact for the Kingdom of God and glorifying the Father in our neck of the woods!

Better Together

It is important to realise that I cannot do what I do without the collaborative efforts of the businesspeople, entrepreneurs and marketplace leaders who served alongside me; men and women who excel in developing their gifts and talents, offer their resources and the fruits of their labour for Kingdom-purpose and challenge my thinking on a daily basis. These people are deeply committed to God and the extension of His Kingdom, while building great businesses which supply resources and position them for influence in every area of society.

Where people come together and align themselves according to the purposes of God, there is not just greater productivity but a supernatural attraction of blessing and favour that results—almost like a magnet.

This is why unity and alignment is so crucial. Where people come together and align themselves according to the purposes of God, there is not just greater productivity but a supernatural attraction of blessing and favour that results—almost like a magnet.

When I was at school, I learned the principle of *magnetism*. During a science class, our teacher instructed us to place iron filings in a jar with a metal rod. Nothing happened. He then instructed us to rub the metal rod with a magnet several times in the same direction, which created an unseen magnetic field. This time, when the rod was placed back in the jar, the iron filings were attracted and stuck tightly to it. Something mysterious had happened to the metal rod as the magnet rubbed against it.

We learned that the particles within the metal rod were originally arranged in different directions. However, the magnet caused the particles to align themselves. This created a force of attraction for the iron filings, which in turn, lined themselves up with those in the rod as they were drawn together by the invisible magnetic field. In order to be attracted, the particles needed to be facing the same direction. The magnet created *alignment*, the alignment created a *force* and the force created *attraction*. This is something I have never forgotten and, as with many of God's natural laws, mirrors a spiritual principle for us to live by.

Unfortunately, too many people within the church and the marketplace alike miss out on the power of this spiritual principle because they are unwilling to let go of their own opinions and rights. Western culture generally celebrates 'my way', 'my beliefs' and 'my dreams'—in essence, 'my right to be different'. When working with others, it is all too easy to let points of disagreement become the focus, but the truth is that there is often so much more that we *can* agree on! When we understand the power of alignment with a common cause, then we realise that some of our personal differences are worth setting aside for the sake of unity and partnership.

I believe that the supernatural favour we have seen in our endeavours in Papua New Guinea is not just the result of my efforts, but rather an example of the power of unity and alignment. Not everyone I work with agrees with everything I believe. It's probably true that many of them would do certain things differently if they were in my shoes. But what we do agree on is the importance of making an impact in a nation that is long-lasting and holistic. This alignment with the vision has enough to bring many influential, gifted and well-resourced people together to achieve something remarkable. As a result, we have seen doors of opportunity open before us that promise to reap a harvest for generations to come.

In other words, if we are going to fulfil our great mandate to win cities for the Kingdom of God, we cannot do it alone. It is only when EVERY believer recognises the critical role they play in the redemption of their sphere of influence that the Body of Christ truly stands up and begins to MOVE as it was called to move and SHINE as it was called to shine! Alone we can only do so much, but TOGETHER, we can win cities!

A Counterculture

So, how do YOU position yourself to shine brightly? How can YOU participate in exploits that are far greater and far more eternally significant than simply making money to build *your* earthly kingdom, day in and day out? How can YOUR spiritual *light* find expression in the natural, day-to-day working culture around you?

I'm glad you asked.

You only have to look at the catch phrases that have been coined to describe the prevailing culture of our world—'rat race', 'dog-eat-dog world', 'every man for himself'—to understand the deep-seated survival mindset of those who navigate these spiritually *dark* places on a daily basis.

Many begin their careers with good intentions to make the world a better place, but eventually yield to the unspoken mantra, "Do whatever it takes to succeed".

Many begin their careers with good intentions to make the world a better place, but eventually yield to the unspoken mantra, "Do whatever it takes to succeed".

I'm sure you will agree that the marketplace is in general, a ruthless and unspiritual environment. If we, as Christians, desire to bring about change, we must embrace and seek to present a *counterculture*—that of the Kingdom of God. It is only when presented with a different and superior culture, that people begin to scrutinise their own and the effect it is having on their lives, legacies and influence. When faced with options, they are positioned to choose for themselves, rather than following the herd mindlessly.

Sadly, many Christians find the idea of resisting the flow of common culture to be too daunting and instead, yield to it in order to survive. Effectively, they choose to *cover their lamp* with a bowl and allow the flame to be hidden or go out, rather than draw unwanted attention and criticism to themselves or their businesses because of their faith. But just as light is counter to darkness, so too our attitude, mindset and behaviour must counter the darkened culture in which we work. Failure to do so sets us up to become 'Sunday Christians', compartmentalising our lives in ways that rob us of peace, integrity and favour.

Of course, we know that fear can be found lurking in darkness and the fast-paced world of business enterprise and supply lines are no different. Everyone is in desperate pursuit of success—as the world defines it—desperately avoiding the rubbish heap of failed business exploits and dead-end ideas. But not all motivation is selfish. The desire to prosper and provide for those that we love is built into the DNA of every human being. God is, Himself, the ultimate provider and has hardwired this same desire into His creation. Fear of failure and the repercussions of our failure on our loved ones, is an incredibly strong motivation. These internal driving fears originate in the mind and are powerful in influencing our actions and choices. Thankfully God offers us the antidote:

> *Therefore do not worry, saying, 'What shall we eat?' or 'What shall we drink?' or 'What shall we wear?' For after all these things the Gentiles seek. For your heavenly Father knows that you need all these things. But seek first the kingdom of God and His righteousness, and all these things shall be added to you.*
> — *Matthew 6:31-33 (NKJV)*

Kings or Dictators?

Unlike those who, in ignorance, chase after the things that they need, believers are challenged to FIRST AND FOREMOST chase after God's Kingdom. While we so often view provision as the *prize* after which we must chase, God instead sees it as the *reward* and *birthright* for pursuing the business of His Kingdom. This is the essence of what it means to think and behave like a king. In the next chapter, we will examine this in more detail, but in the meantime, ask yourself this question: Does a king worry about what he will eat or the clothes he will wear? I think not. A king's sole responsibility and concern is to rule over his kingdom. The rest is taken care of as part of his royal inheritance.

In contrast, a *dictator*, without the security of royal bloodline, takes what he needs and wants by force. He must then protect what is his, watching his back at all times in case another more ambitious dictator-in-waiting should rise up and challenge his authority. This is the prevailing mindset of many who work in the marketplace. It is an insecure existence with fear at the helm. It is my belief that many Christian professionals today simply lack the understanding of who they really are and what God has called them to. Without this knowledge, we are destined to take our place in the boxing ring of corporate life, hoping to be the last man standing.

I want so much more for you. It's time that the Church raised kings and queens to rule over the marketplace and supply lines to our cities—free of the limitations and bondages of a dictator mindset. To do this, we must focus on transforming our thinking and building our lives on the truth of our identity in Christ. Only then will our actions and decisions align with God's Kingdom and usher in the untouchable success and deep fulfilment that is our birthright as sons and daughters of God.

It's time to rule.

BE

I hope I am beginning to convince you that you were created for a far greater purpose than acquiring wealth for personal comfort and influence for personal recognition. Hopefully something is stirring in you right now, urging you to take stock of where you are at and open your heart and eyes to the greater calling of God for your life.

If you desire to be great for God, you, like me, may need a mindset *shift*. As the old saying goes, "The definition of insanity is doing the same thing over and over again and expecting different results." Although I agree with this entirely, notice that the focus is on *doing*. What would make a person DO the same things over and over again, hoping for a different result? The answer, I believe, is that they have not taken the time to examine and adjust their THINKING.

It is commonly accepted that our actions, reactions and choices find their foundations in our thinking.

THINK ➡ DO

But I believe that there is one more component missing from this simple life equation that has the power to change both our thoughts and actions. Simply put, our thoughts originate from our conviction of who we are: our *identity*. I like to call this our BEING.

BE ➡ THINK ➡ DO

Our journey towards living more fruitful, prosperous, meaningful and generationally significant lives begins with a defining revelation of who we are.

Our identity is formed and shaped over the course of our lives through our culture, experiences, relationships, media, work and the environment in which we live. Daily, we receive an overwhelming amount of messaging telling us to define ourselves according to an external set of measures and a societal value system. But I wonder what would happen if we began to reject these ever-changing and subjective criteria, and instead, based our identity on what God—our Creator—says about us.

Psychologists have a lot to say on the subject, but I want to hone in on one simple truth about our identity that is revealed in God's Word and has the power to radically transform our lives. What is that truth?

You are ROYALTY.

If you are tempted to roll your eyes at this point, stay with me.

Have you ever wondered why we are captivated by royalty? Love them or hate them; we are drawn, even from a young age, to stories about royals. Regardless of our culture, status or background, most of us as children dream of being a prince or princess. These dreams typically come crashing down as we grow older and come to terms with our reality, but where do those desires originate?

A Royal Bloodline

The biblical account of the creation of humanity makes it clear that we were created in the image of the King of Kings, born to be royal and *commissioned* to rule.

> **God blessed them and said to them, "Be fruitful and increase in number; fill the earth and subdue it. Rule over the fish in the sea and the birds in the sky and over every living creature that moves on the ground."**
> **— Genesis 1:28 (NIV)**

While the curse of sin temporarily separated us from our Heavenly Father, deep down in its soul, humanity has never fully forgotten that royalty is in our blood.

> *But you are God's chosen treasure—priests who are kings, a spiritual "nation" set apart as God's devoted ones. He called you out of darkness to experience his marvelous light, and now he claims you as his very own. He did this so that you would broadcast his glorious wonders throughout the world.*
>
> *— 1 Peter 2:9 (TPT)*

Our royal identity is irrefutable. When we surrender our lives to Christ, we are restored to the fullness of the image of God. We are re-born and adopted into the royal bloodline of God's family and recommissioned to rule and reign on Earth.

> *But to all who believed him and accepted him, he gave the right to become children of God.*
>
> *—John 1:12 (NLT)*

As if being royal by re-birth is not enough, we are also royal by *marriage*. Just as a bride takes on her husband's name, we, the Church of Jesus Christ, are His bride and have taken on His Name!

> *For your Maker is your husband,*
> *The Lord of hosts is His name;*
> *And your Redeemer is the Holy One of Israel;*
> *He is called the God of the whole earth.*
>
> *— Isaiah 54:5 (NKJV)*

We should EXPECT our circumstances to change as a result of carrying God's family Name. The spouses and family members of celebrities are famous, not because of their own achievements, but because of the *name* they carry. This name affords them privileges that they would otherwise not deserve. This is also true of us as Christians. We carry a royal name, the name of Jesus Christ— the King of Kings. This name has the power to open closed doors, access unlimited resources and exercise authority in domains where we would otherwise have no authority.

An Empty Throne

The enemy is especially aware of our restored position and its entitlements, and because he cannot dethrone us, he focuses on convincing us to walk away from our throne by keeping us blinded to who we really are. The truth is that kingdom rule is never just for the benefit of a king, but for his realm and his subjects. In other words, when we live without a revelation of our true identity, not only do we miss out on our royal privileges, but others miss out as well. Worse still, unwanted identities can quickly step in to fill the vacuum of leadership that our *abdication* creates.

> *"An empty throne is a usurper's invitation."*
>
> — *Dr Clayton Coombs*

So, you are a KING (men and women alike), but if you don't occupy the throne that God has given you, somebody or something else will!

When we begin to think of ourselves as God thinks of us, we should expect that revelation to stimulate significant change in the way we see life and make choices. It is inevitable that we will begin to carry AUTHORITY—a quality that is invisible yet tangibly felt by those around us—and to attract wealth and favour at levels we have never known before. In saying that, I'm sure you will have experienced first-hand, that not all wealth and favour is of God and ultimately beneficial in our lives. It is critical, as kings, to know how to discern the difference.

Do you not know that in a race all the runners run, but only one gets the prize? Run in such a way as to get the prize. Everyone who competes in the games goes into strict training. They do it to get a crown that will not last, but we do it to get a crown that will last forever. Therefore I do not run like someone running aimlessly; I do not fight like a boxer beating the air. No, I strike a blow to my body and make it my slave so that after I have preached to others, I myself will not be disqualified for the prize.

— 1 Corinthians 9:24-27 (NIV)

This verse has always intrigued me. I remember first reading it and being amazed at the idea that as Christians, we can and should be seeking rewards for our labours. However, kingly thinking recognises that the prizes God has in mind are not the transient rewards of mere financial success, but rather, *eternal* rewards.

True Success

Long after the memory of our moment on Earth has passed, we will still be celebrating and revelling in the only measure of true and lasting *success*—the souls of human beings that were restored to the Father, and the legacy of godly businesses and cultural institutions that were restored, redeemed and repurposed for Kingdom influence. Only *you* can choose whether or not you will focus on the eternal or get caught up in the pursuit of personal comfort and significance in the eyes of man.

The stakes are high and the consequences are eternal. I hope you choose *like a king*.

Our understanding of who we are in the eyes of God extends even further beyond our relationship with Him and the entitlements and responsibilities of our birthright. In order to rule and reign victoriously and successfully over our assigned territory, we must understand and accept the uniqueness of our gifting and purpose—those things that God intentionally instilled in us before we took our first breath.

> *Before I formed you in the womb I knew you,*
> *before you were born I set you apart...*
>   *— Jeremiah 1:5 (NIV)*

> *For we are God's handiwork, created in Christ Jesus to do*
> *good works, which God prepared in advance for us to do.*
>   *— Ephesians 2:10 (NIV)*

I love the way Bishop TD Jakes, in his book entitled, *Identity*, describes the importance of living with divine purpose in mind. I hope that his wisdom serves as a wake-up call to us all:

> *You can live in this world and make all the money you could ever dream of and be as beautiful as you want and be as educated as you please and accomplish whatever you want to, but if you die without accomplishing your purpose, you are a failure, a reject, and a fool.*
>   *— Bishop T. D. Jakes*

Maximising Strength

Living life with divine purpose begins with maximising the strengths that God has placed in you to enable you to fulfil your unique calling. That doesn't mean that we cannot learn and grow, but that we have been equipped by God with all that we need to walk successfully in our divine purpose.

His divine power has given us everything we need for a godly life through our knowledge of him who called us by his own glory and goodness.

— *2 Peter 1:3 (NIV)*

It is our gifting that acts like a compass to help set the course of our lives, while it is the faithful guidance of the Holy Spirit that keeps us from wandering from the path to our destiny.

In 1 Corinthians 9:26 (ESV), Paul says, "I do not run aimlessly, I do not box as one beating the air". Paul is not prepared to live out his life *hoping* that he will one day hit the mark and win the race. Instead, he is urging us to live out our lives with intentionally and purpose, honing our gifts and talents with great discipline so that every 'punch' finds its mark. Identifying our unique gifts and talents is part of the process of making contact with our destiny. It also helps us stay in the lane that will take us there without diversion or distraction.

When I was in school, I had really long legs which helped me run with speed. I remember competing in races and being so careful not to step over the line and into the next person's lane because that meant instant disqualification. Not only would veering outside my designated zone lead me off course, but it would also interfere with another runner's ability to run their race, causing potential collision and injury. It took *discipline* to stay on course and this is wisdom that can and should be applied to every area of our lives, including our business.

Networking is the catchcry of many business training seminars. The general idea is to 'cover your bases' in business by connecting with as many influential business people as you can and using those connections to diversify so that you have options when challenges present. Seems wise, but notice what is hidden below the surface: fear, self-doubt and insecurity—traits that are rarely displayed in the life of a true king.

The most important person you need to be in relationship with is Jesus. This relationship reveals our identity, breeds security and correctly orders all our other relationships by replacing fear with love.

The simple truth is that you are most powerful when you know who you are, what you are skilled in and which lane you are called to run in. It's called FOCUS. A 'just in case' mentality will lead to distraction and comparison that will in turn take you off course and onto the path of unnecessary injury to yourself and to others.

I have listened to too many stories of businesspeople who had so many 'irons in the fire' that they were rendered completely ineffective. Instead of building a reputation for knowing and perfecting their product and standing as an authority in the marketplace, their diversity led them to occupy the dreaded place of average in the field, competing with experts who had instead chosen to focus and excel within the boundaries of their strengths.

The simple truth is that you are most powerful when you know who you are, what you are skilled in and which lane you are called to run in. It's called FOCUS.

> *A man's gift makes room for him, and brings him before*
> *great men.*
> *— Proverbs 18:16 (NIV)*

Notice that the *gift* that brings a man into environments of greatness is HIS gift—not someone else's. If we are to think like kings, we cannot become distracted by comparing ourselves to others which only leads to fear and insecurity. Understanding who God has called us to be releases us to focus on the gifts on OUR lives, trusting that He will supply everything we need to see us win our race and take the prize.

Many years have passed since my wife and I pastored a church in Western Australia. It was an incredibly fruitful season of our lives and one we look back on with a great sense of joy—not to say that we did not face some significant challenges. Towards the end of that season, I was also leading the Australian Christian Churches movement in our state—another challenging but fulfilling role. For people looking on, I must have appeared to be running successfully in my lane, 'kicking goals' as we would say in Australia. But what people did not see was a growing sense from God that this was *not* my lane to run and that He was about to change my course.

I struggled for two years to come to terms with what God was trying to tell me and was bombarded with thoughts of what might happen if I let go of my current success in order to head off into the unknown in pursuit of God's will. My wife and I finally surrendered and left our church to relocate our lives to Melbourne, Australia, under the leadership of Senior Pastors Russell and Sam Evans. Once again, from the outside looking in, it must have seemed like a *demotion*. I was no longer a senior pastor leading a movement at a state level, but now a team member of a large staff under the leadership of another.

I won't lie by saying that the transition was smooth. There was a lot of dying to old dreams and visions that needed to happen, and dying is never pleasant. But through it all, I knew God had called me to greatness, as He has each one of you, and that I was in a preparation phase for new levels of authority and influence. God was re-writing the script I had written for my own life—re-routing the satellite navigation system (my thinking) that was steering me off-course. I, like you, had a choice—to hold onto control or yield to the will of God. I had to stop worshipping at the altar of my own ambition, and instead lay that ambition on the altar before God. Perhaps you too need to ask the Holy Spirit if there are some ambitions that you need to lay down.

Retrospect is an amazing thing and looking back now, I can see that God always leads us forward and higher, even when our limited thinking leaves us feeling like we are going backwards.

By God's grace, I have now entered a stage of authority and influence that I had only dreamt about. In my current role as Planetshakers International Director, I have had the incredible privilege of working with heads of nations to see God's Kingdom advance. I have partnered with billionaires and seen millions of dollars directed into Kingdom endeavours. I have overseen food relief for thousands of people caught in the crisis of a global pandemic and strategised with giants of the faith on how to champion the cause of the Holy Spirit on Earth. I have called great men and women, saved and unsaved, my personal friends and travelled the world to minister in and support local churches. I tell you this, again not to brag, but to recognise that God has released me to have far greater influence and impact under the covering of my senior pastor than I ever would have had if I had resisted His leading and held on to the position and influence that I once had.

I encourage you to find your own particular lane and run in it because that is the place where you will be empowered and released to succeed at levels you have only dreamt of. Don't disqualify yourself for the prize by trying to assume somebody else's identity or operate in their uniquely anointed calling.

Don't disqualify yourself for the prize by trying to assume somebody else's identity or operate in their uniquely anointed calling.

Right now, I could so easily be working hard back in Western Australia, building my own little empire and convincing myself that I was doing it for God. Though it has been costly in every way, following the higher call of God for me personally has been the most fruitful and rewarding adventure of my life. But it started with a challenge to my thinking that, when settled, led to me becoming a *kingly* version of Neil Smith—the one God created me to be.

Before we move on to discussing our *thinking* in greater detail, may I urge you to take the time to examine YOUR identity? Do you see yourself as a king with entitlements that surpass your wildest expectations? Do you know beyond a shadow of a doubt that your provision is a given when your focus shifts to seeking God's Kingdom and ruling over your assigned territory? Have you identified and accepted your own unique shape—the intentionality of a loving Father who dreamed you and your destiny into being and fully equipped you for Kingdom purpose?

Or do you see yourself as just another person trying to stay afloat in a self-seeking, broken world?

I call out the king inside of you. It's time to take your throne.

CHAPTER 2 BE

3

THINK

Now that I have reminded you who you are in Christ—a *king* of royal bloodline, with a royal calling and royal entitlements— it's now time to explore how this identity will affect your thinking and in turn, your actions, decisions and ultimately, your success.

In the early days of this evolving revelation of kingship in my life, God orchestrated divine appointments with several significant businesspeople and industry leaders who I would go on to befriend and who would help set me on course to become the man and leader I am today. I valued and respected these relationships and resolved to learn as much FROM them as I was imparting TO them. As a result, my thinking was challenged, stretched and enriched as God gifted me with the ability to relate well to both marketplace and ministry-minded people.

One of the people who deeply impacted my life was a successful resort and property developer in Asia—Dato' Edward Ong. Throughout our ongoing relationship, Edward gave me privileged insight into the thinking of a successful Christian businessman who was wholly committed to both business AND his local church.

On one occasion, Edward ran a week-long course for Christian business people in his Kota Kinabalu Resort and invited me to attend to offer spiritual counsel and advice to the delegates. This opportunity immersed me even deeper into the world of Christian professionals and unexpectedly re-ignited my own passion for business in the process. Though I knew that my primary call was to ministry and not the pursuit of personal wealth, I was very aware that God was birthing something new in me that would be significant and fruitful for His Kingdom. I would later come to realise that this inner stirring would preempt a revolution in the relationship between the marketplace and church communities that would lead to new and greater levels of Kingdom advancement than I had ever seen before.

As I thought about what I was observing, God began to speak clearly to me about the importance of our thinking. I began to realise that no matter how great the gift of God and call on a person's life, every man and woman is subject to live within the boundaries of their own thinking.

No matter how great the gift of God and call on a person's life, every man and woman is subject to live within the boundaries of their own thinking.

For as he thinks in his heart, so is he.
— *Proverbs 23:7 (NKJV)*

Proverbs 23:7 has made a huge impact in my life. I now understand, with increasing revelation, that what we truly believe about ourselves (the thinking of our hearts) will determine WHO we become, and in turn, what we DO with our lives, skills and resources. In short, our successes and achievements in life will reflect our fundamental thoughts and beliefs. The urgent question then is, What is the source of our thoughts and beliefs? The answer—as we have already discussed in the previous chapter—is found in our *identity*. It is from a deep place of internal belief about who we are that our thoughts are born, established and begin to exercise influence in our lives.

The Orphan M.O.

I could see many incredible men and women in marketplace careers who had so much potential for great Kingdom exploits, being led around like slaves by the culture and values of their working environments. They were operating like orphans—working tirelessly to get ahead of the pack and survive in the world. It was as if they had forgotten who they were— *heirs* with Christ with an assured inheritance, called and equipped to take dominion over their assigned territory. They were anxious and uncertain of the future, and ultimately, what they believed about themselves was being fulfilled before their eyes.

The truth is, what we believe about ourselves is a *game-changer* and the genesis of a thought life that either ushers us into our divine destiny, or keeps us trapped under the ceiling of human reasoning and expectation.

> **Now if we are children, then we are heirs—heirs of God and co-heirs with Christ.**
>
> — *Romans 8:17 (NIV)*

While most Christians understand that we are children of a King, we must begin thinking like that King in order to prepare for the moment when we are called to step up and rule over our assigned realm. The certainty of inheriting a natural fortune leads to a different level of thinking to that of an orphaned child who does not expect to receive anything. The same is true in the spiritual. Along with the privilege of inheritance comes the responsibility to steward that inheritance in a way that honours the one who gifts it to us.

As Christians and children of the King of Kings, we are *obligated* to push past the limited thinking of an orphan; to move beyond *surviving* and into the higher calling of exercising dominion and authority. We must step up to the highest position where our light can be most powerfully seen by all who come into contact with us—whether up close or from a distance.

If you are looking for business principles or motivational input, I'm afraid you are reading the wrong book. There are a plethora of self-help resources out there that can help you develop the skills of business and industry. I am calling instead on those who want to stretch beyond the limitations of our current understanding and up to a higher level where we embrace *calling* above *occupation*. I am speaking to those who are willing to prioritise eternal outcomes over temporal ones and who are driven by God-given purpose rather than earthly success. I am aware that this kind of person is rare, but I am hoping and believing that YOU will join the ranks!

The King's Kingdom

Every king has a kingdom.

Let's talk about the *Kingdom of God* and our own realm of authority that lies within its boundaries.

> **But seek first his kingdom and his righteousness, and all these things will be given to you as well.**
> — *Matthew 6:33 (NIV)*

So what does it really mean to seek after God's Kingdom? What does that entail in our lives on a daily basis? Can this seeking be scheduled into our busy lives or ticked off our 'to do' list at the end of a gruelling day running the business or working a job? If we are not careful, pursuing God and His Kingdom can quickly feel like yet another burden to be added to the workload or another reason to feel guilty or like a failure. But I don't believe this is the case.

I believe that when God speaks of His Kingdom, He is specifically targeting our THINKING. The Bible makes it really clear that our minds are the battleground of our spirits and that our thought life is directly responsible for our actions and the outcomes of our lives. As such, our thinking must be continually renewed in order to align with God's Word and our divine identity as kings. This will keep us on track in accomplishing our God-given destiny.

> **Do not conform to the pattern of this world, but be transformed by the renewing of your mind. Then you will be able to test and approve what God's will is—his good, pleasing and perfect will.**
> — *Romans 12:2 (NIV)*

In my many years of pastoring businesspeople and professionals, I have noticed a pattern of very limited thinking that is common. Many operate with the daily mindset of "I've got to get up in the morning and make money so I can feed my family, pay those bills, pay for that holiday I promised my spouse, give my child the gift they've been dreaming of... etc." We are consumed with what we *need* in the short term, and this can become a daily grind and perpetual routine that never ends and weighs heavily on our shoulders. This kind of thinking, though it appears noble, needs transforming. We were called to more than survival. But this kind of limited thinking will not suddenly change on its own. It must be challenged and replaced with a new mindset that leads to new results. Transformed thinking is the process of learning and progressing by hearing the voice of God as He directs us in our lives. It involves constant CHANGE—something that can be challenging to some who prefer predictability.

Transformed thinking requires an accurate revelation of who we are in Christ—our true IDENTITY as kings and priests, called to bring God glory by shining light everywhere we are assigned to rule.

> *To Him who loved us and washed us from our sins in His own blood, and has made us kings and priests to His God and Father, to Him be glory and dominion forever and ever. Amen.*
>
> *— Revelation 1:5-6 (NKJV)*

Even saying the word *king* evokes an image of someone who is not ordinary in any way. Kings are powerful, wealthy individuals—born to rule. That's what makes them different from any other individual who comes into power by force or election. *Dictators*, for example, must work hard to take and keep their place, often by plundering and undermining the authority of another. They have a mindset of self-preservation, ambition and control, and their leadership lasts only as long as it takes the next conqueror to arise. You don't need to look far to see this attitude outworked in the modern day culture of business and industry. Those who lead like dictators in the marketplace may appear to be in positions of strength one day, but find themselves ousted by hostile takeovers the next. Ultimately, theirs is an *insecure* existence that relies on constant efforts to ensure the compliance of all around them.

Not so for a true king!

A true king is born into both wealth and authority. They do not lie awake at night worrying about resources or scheming how to overthrow another or win the approval of the people. Wealth, authority and purpose is GIFTED to them because of who they are and the bloodline they were born into. All that is needed is that they *grow into* their position and prepare themselves for the moment they are called to take the throne. Much time and resource is invested into their development and there are many who advise them along the way.

A true king does not lie awake at night worrying about resources or scheming how to overthrow another.

Make no mistake: such a position comes with enormous responsibility and hard work. Because they have an innate understanding of their royalty, kings willingly submit themselves to training, hard work and discipline to cultivate the skills and mindsets necessary to govern a kingdom. History has shown that some upcoming kings *baulk* at the personal cost of their impending sovereignty and fail to take their place as they were born to do. But before we criticise them, I'm sure we would all opt for privilege without the burden of hard work and responsibility, if given the chance.

As we talked about in the last chapter, we were gifted with *Kingdom authority* by God when we were grafted into His family through salvation. The question is, do we understand what that means for our lives and how that relates to being a Christian working in the marketplace? This is what I hope to unpack in the following chapters, but it MUST begin with the way that we think!

Core Beliefs

The concept of *core beliefs* reveals some powerful truths about the way that we see ourselves and the impact that it has on our lives. Core beliefs are basic beliefs that we have about the world and subconsciously hold to be absolute truths. They are beliefs that we accept without question, that in turn, inform our thoughts, influence our reactions and determine how we process information and perceive situations.

No matter what core beliefs currently govern your thinking and how you came to establish them in the first place, I hope you can see the critical importance of intentionally discovering them, challenging them and, if necessary, creating new ones that reflect the truth of God's Word in our lives. This is what the Apostle Paul refers to as being "transformed by the renewing of the mind." Simply put, we must take the time to intentionally address our thinking if we want to change the outcomes in our life. We can all do this. It's free of charge, but requires a commitment to change and absolute honesty with ourselves.

So I ask you today, What are you thinking about most? What does your thinking reveal about how you see yourself? How is that thinking limiting your fruitfulness in life and business? Do you think like a king? Do you approach life with the confident expectation that you will step into a place of authority, influence and dominion when your 'for such a time as this' moment arrives? Do you see your current failures as an integral part of your kingly development, knowing that they cannot undermine your future destiny unless you allow them to? Are you focussed on honing your gifts and talents in readiness for your moment of significance?

Alternatively, do you have a core belief that is undermining your true potential? Do you see yourself as the 'underdog'? Are you constantly on edge worrying about your future? Do you live with a persistent nagging feeling of failure? Do you feel the need to be on guard for opportunities to undermine others in order to get your share of the market? Do you see every other person in your industry as a competitor? Do you worry that you are not good enough at your job to expect success? Do you have many 'irons in the fire' to protect your business against unforeseen disaster? Do you approach business with a 'fight or die', 'struggle to the death' mindset?

A king knows, from childhood, that the throne will be his when the time is right. He does not strive to position himself for kingship. He IS the king—whether in training or in ruling.

> **Now then, I say, for as long a time as the heir is a child, he is no different from a servant, although he be lord of all...**
> — *Galatians 4:1 (AFV)*

This is a core belief and mindset that we must adopt and practise if we are to flourish in life and in the ministry of business. Though we may not feel like we have reached the place of *dominion* yet, we MUST live with the confident assurance that we have been gifted a portion of an earthly kingdom so that we can exert influence and direct supply for the extension of God's Kingdom. In God's eyes we are kings— heirs to the throne and guaranteed success (when the timing is right). It is only our own mindset of who we are that can keep us thinking and behaving like paupers, striving to obtain a position of influence and success that has already been generously gifted to us by re-birth and marriage.

A young man in our church comes to mind when I think of the impact our thinking can have on who we become. He got connected to our church through our university ministry and gave his life to Jesus before starting in business. He came from an influential family of stature and I immediately noticed something different about his thinking to others of his age.

Seeing the clear call of God on his life, I began to act as one of his mentors and was privileged to journey with him. Prior to experiencing any personal success in business, he believed that he was called and destined to make significant amounts of money to help resource the local church and the Kingdom of God. When he completed university, he took a tech job at Fuji Xerox. I later found out that he gave away his first full year's salary, believing that living another year in a student-like state wouldn't hurt him and that giving God the first-fruits of his crops would position him for God's favour and protection over future income. I was moved by his radical faith and lack of concern for how he would make ends meet during that season.

There was something unique about the way this young man thought about life and success and I believe it came from a place of innate security, having been raised as an heir to a natural inheritance from his earthly father. It was therefore natural for him to transfer this same feeling of absolute security to his Heavenly Father's affairs. There was no limitation in his thinking that prevented him from stepping into the fullness of his destiny. He simply believed that if God had promised him resource and success for Kingdom purpose, then that was exactly what would come.

And he was right. Just a few years later, he is by far one of the most successful and influential men in our church—now the Managing Director of a large, international property development company that he and his wife founded. He simply *became* what he believed (and thought) he would become.

More recently, this same young man was serving as a VIP driver at our men's conference. In itself, this was incredible to witness. A successful businessman, accustomed to being treated with honour, humbled himself to serve others. Once again, he was absolutely secure in who he was called to be, regardless of the task set before him. Unwavering in his commitment to putting God first, he made it a non-negotiable priority for he and his family to attend our church's annual conference and serve every year.

This particular year, I noticed that his wife was not present for one of the conference sessions and was told that his company had won a prestigious industry award—Annual REA Excellence Awards: Game Changer of the Year. Instead of attending the award ceremony himself, he sent his wife to receive it on his behalf and continued driving VIPs to and from the conference. Alarmed, I asked him why he hadn't told me earlier so I could replace him as a driver and free him up to receive his award. He humbly reminded me that the reason for his success in the first place was because he had honoured God first, so why would he stop now? Astounding, but not surprising. His radical, yet simple mindset was fast-tracking him into his destiny! He had learned to position himself during his time of preparation, so that he could one day handle the weight of what God had called him to—a territory within God's Kingdom over which to rule and have dominion.

If this story inspires you—and it should—why not honestly examine your own thinking today? Ask the Holy Spirit to help you identify the barriers and break them down so that you can begin thinking like a king and step into the fullness of your destiny and purpose. Recognise that God has set aside a portion of His Kingdom for you to rule and reign over, and He will order your steps to accomplish this in your life!

Thinking > Doing

I finish our discussion on the power of your thinking by presenting an interesting fact that I hope inspires you as much as it did me when I discovered it. The reality is that in society today, more is paid for what a person *thinks* than what they actually *do*. What do I mean by that? Well, a large percentage of the total wage bill of large corporations is paid to a small percentage of the top executives. In fact, in the United States, CEOs are paid roughly 278 times the average wage. This often causes public outrage as it seems to lack equality and disadvantage the hard-working, grassroots employees that run the daily affairs of the corporation. What most don't understand is that it is the small percentage of employees, like CEOs, that generate the *ideas*. These ideas are what increases the profitability of the corporation. In short, their salary reflects the revenue they attract. It is their minds that are the 'hot property'. Most people can get a job done if they have the skills, but not everyone can generate an idea that will radically change the landscape of a business.

> *"Money doesn't make money, ideas do."*
>
> — *Dato' Edward Ong*

Many business people that I have met over the years have limited the potential of their company by stubbornly upholding the rigid belief that they must be hands-on at all times to maintain control. Essentially, they reduce themselves to a baseline employee and leave no time or room to allow themselves to conduct research, consult mentors and dream of new ideas that can launch them into greater levels of success. This is the privilege of kings: empowering others to oversee the core business while they concern themselves with the critical responsibility of high-end governance.

Stage 1 in transforming your thinking is seeing yourself in a new light: entrusting others with the tasks of the business while you focus on 'big-picture' thinking and planning. A worker, on the other hand, is focussed on their pay slip—hoping for a pay rise or promotion to advance them to a higher level. They wake up each day to a list of tasks and meetings to tick off the 'to-do' list, while the thinker wakes up to the question, How can I stimulate new business? The way each thinks is radically different. Although it is important to work hard in everything our hands find to do (Colossians 3:23), it is not the same as being limited by a *worker's mentality* that can be a great obstacle to our thinking and in turn our success.

Your thinking is making you the person that you are. If you do not regularly set aside time with God to assess, challenge and retrain your thinking, you will never be positioned to hear the very God-ideas and strategies that could launch your business and personal life to levels you have only dreamed about.

So, the question remains, "Do you believe you are a king, called by God to sit in a place of authority and dominion over an assigned patch of earthly kingdom, in order to extend and advance His divine Kingdom?

SCAN & WATCH

If the answer is yes, are you thinking like one?

DO

For we are God's handiwork, created in Christ Jesus to do good works, which God prepared in advance for us to do.

— Ephesians 2:10 (NIV) —

I hope the reality of your royal identity is beginning to sink in and take root in your mind, invading your thoughts and generating fresh possibilities in God. I hope you are beginning to see clearly that the walls, bars and ceilings you have operated within are imaginary limitations that you can so easily break free of and step into a new level of revelation and divine purpose.

I am reminded of a story that I heard years ago.

Conditioned to Be Contained

As the story goes, in years gone by, circus elephants used to be trained in a certain way from infancy so that when they reached adulthood, they could be safely controlled around humans. While small and relatively powerless, baby elephants would be chained by their leg to a stake in the ground to limit their movements. Infant elephants were not strong enough to pull out the stake and escape, and when they tried, they would be struck with a whip or cane which forced them to comply.

As the elephants grew and became vastly superior in size and strength, they failed to realise that they could now easily pull out the small stake and make their escape. The whip and cane had no real power to control any grown elephant that decided that it was time to break free, yet they remained compliant and trapped within the imaginary limitations of their own thinking that had been established and reinforced with repetition and discipline during their formative years. The feel of a chain around their leg—even one that was not even attached to a stake—was enough to control the movements of a huge and potentially dangerous animal.

There is a powerful lesson to be learned here. Just because our identity, thinking and behaviour have been intentionally conditioned by powerful influences—mostly during the formative years of our lives and careers—it does not mean that we cannot outgrow this state and at any time, break out and begin to operate at a new level!

It is my prayer that you would stop identifying as an orphan and step up confidently into your rightful position as son or daughter of the King. Whatever lies are acting as limitations to keep you contained and moving in circles, please take this moment to break free of them. Your divine purpose awaits your breakthrough!

Now we come to the 'meaty' part of this journey—the DOING. This is what we all really want to know. How can we change the outcomes of our lives and walk in new levels of favour, prosperity and fruitfulness? Well, to me the answer is simple. It all comes back to our PURPOSE.

We have already discussed that as kings (or kings-in-waiting), our thinking must change to reflect the reality of our mandate. We must not allow ourselves to be distracted with day-to-day tasks that we can empower others to do. We do not need to live with constant underlying anxiety about how we will make ends meet, because we know we have full access to the unlimited resources of God's Kingdom. We no longer need to feel threatened by perceived competitors or worried that we could lose it all if we do not remain vigilant and on the offence.

We do not need to live with constant underlying anxiety about how we will make ends meet, because we know we have full access to the unlimited resources of God's Kingdom.

If we are to operate as kings, we must let go of all of these distractions, limitations and fears, and instead, intentionally focus in on our highest calling—to RULE over our assigned territory.

Attracting vs Chasing

I was born in England where people are very familiar with the concept of *royalty*. The current Queen of England, Her Majesty, Queen Elizabeth II, is an excellent example of what it is to be royal and fully committed to your purpose. For this queen, purpose is considered to be divinely mandated and has remained relatively unaffected by decades of cultural change in her nation. It is safe to say that she is driven by a strong sense of cause and responsibility for the people over which she rules.

One very familiar image that comes to mind is the Queen sitting at her desk each day and opening the 'Red Box'. These famous red boxes are managed by Her Majesty's Private Secretary and are full of important letters, cabinet documents, telegrams and state papers that must be read, approved and signed off. The Queen must deal with the issues contained in the Red Box every single day, with the only exception being Christmas Day.

I think this routine provides us valuable insight into the mindset of someone who is operating in the fullness of her royal identity. The Queen does not seek out tasks or pull up her sleeves in the kitchen alongside the maids and chefs. She simply sits down in her authority and waits for the tasks that specifically require her attention to come to her. These tasks demand her absolute commitment and focus as her response to each one allows others to move forward and uphold her kingdom on her behalf. She is crucial in the chain of command and takes the responsibility of her royal position very seriously, knowing that her decisions will affect the countless lives of the people over whom she rules.

Biblically speaking, ancient kings operated in a very similar way. 1 Kings 3:16-28 tells the powerful story of King Solomon whose purpose was to administer wisdom in his kingdom. When two women brought one baby to him, both claiming to be the child's mother, we see King Solomon resolve the issue masterfully, leaving all of Israel in awe.

Solomon sat down in his authority and the issues came to him. Empowered with divine wisdom, He attracted those in need of help. Having spent much time in the Presence of God, worshipping and sacrificing, learning the ways of his father (King David) and of the kingdom, and requesting wisdom from God to govern his people, Solomon was ready to receive a supernatural solution for this complex natural problem. He was in the right position with the right mindset, and received the download of wisdom from Heaven that he needed to govern justly.

But what about ordinary people like you and I in the Bible? What examples can we find of people who operated with a kingly identity and mindset and, in so doing, attracted their God-given purpose?

The first who comes to mind is Joseph. We are told that as a young man, Joseph had a dream about occupying a position of authority and influence. When he shared that dream with those around him, they tried to contain and define him by his natural circumstances—being the youngest and least significant son among his siblings. Sold into slavery, he did not have the opportunity to chase after his dream of ruling, but instead simply operated out of a strong sense of purpose in every setting he found himself. He was by nature a *ruler*, even when his circumstances defined him as a *slave* and as such, began to attract opportunities to himself— interpreting dreams in prison and serving in the household of Potiphar. In the eyes of those around him, he was a nobody, but Joseph knew he was destined to rule nonetheless. By serving and using his gift of dream interpretation, he was ready and positioned to seize opportunities as they presented themselves, eventually occupying the position of authority and influence that God had revealed to him as a boy.

To unspiritual eyes, Joseph's story reads more like one of accidentally stumbling into one's destiny. But to those of us who know God, His fingerprints can be seen everywhere! Joseph's story started with a dream and ended with the fulfilment of that dream. The journey in between was orchestrated—step-by-step—by God Himself...for HIS glory! All that was required of Joseph was to believe he was who God said he was, to excel in his gifts and to step into rulership when the opportunity presented itself. God asks the same of us today.

Consider Nehemiah for a moment. Not many of us are very familiar with Nehemiah and yet he was instrumental in rebuilding and re-establishing Jerusalem following the Babylonian exile. At the time of his sudden catapult into historical significance, Nehemiah was serving a foreign king in Persia as his cup-bearer. The cup-bearer had the job of testing a king's drinks for poison and would have been regarded as one of the king's closest advisors and thoroughly trustworthy. Nehemiah was not a spiritual leader or prophet, but a man of practical skills whose fervent prayer life triggered great change.

During his time of captivity in the palace, he learned all that he could about governance and leadership and earned the trust of his earthly king. His excellent and loyal service won him favour in the eyes of the king who later facilitated Nehemiah's God-given purpose.

When he heard about the predicament of Jerusalem and how the city remained vulnerable to bandits, gangs and wild animals because the wall surrounding it had broken down, Nehemiah decided to step up and take action. After seeking God fervently for a plan, when the opportunity arrived, Nehemiah instigated this plan and stepped into the higher purpose God had for his life.

Despite being a servant in foreign captivity, Nehemiah's understanding of his true royal identity emboldened him to respond confidently when the Persian king asked him, "What do you request?" In that moment, Nehemiah did not merely ask to be given leave to go and rebuild the wall, but dared to request that the king write letters to other authorities so that he would have freedom of passage and all of the materials required for the project. Nehemiah did not stop at requesting building materials for the rebuilding project, but went so far as to boldly ask the King to supply for the building of his own house!

> *And may I have a letter to Asaph, keeper of the royal park, so he will give me timber to make beams for the gates of the citadel by the temple and for the city wall and for the residence I will occupy?" And because the gracious hand of my God was on me, the king granted my requests.*
>
> *— Nehemiah 2:8 (NIV)*

This is the kind of boldness that we naturally operate in when we understand who we are and whose we are!

As Nehemiah oversaw the huge project of rebuilding the wall, we see him confidently leading the people in the task. He was not afraid of the threats that presented themselves as they built, knowing that God would enable Him to complete his purpose despite the opposition.

No matter what was going on in his life at the time, Nehemiah understood who he was and harnessed every opportunity to grow, excel and prepare for his God-given purpose. When the opportunity arrived, he took hold of it and ran with all of his might. What followed his decision to step up? All of the provision and protection of God that he would ever need to complete the task.

Solomon, Joseph and Nehemiah are all great examples of opportunity, protection and resource being attracted to PURPOSE. The reality is that when you understand your identity as a king and begin to live in your purpose, you will not need to chase after opportunities or resources. They will find YOU. An example of this that comes to mind involves the songwriting business of Planetshakers.

Right Place, Right Time

Some years ago, during a staff prayer meeting, I noticed one of our young musicians caught in his own world, deep in thought and staring into the air. I could see his hands moving—as if playing an invisible keyboard—and I could almost hear the cogs ticking over in his mind. I went to him and quietly asked if he was ok, to which he answered, "Yes, I'm just getting a song". Realising that he was having a 'creative' moment, I left him to his weirdness and watched as he quietly whispered a few words into his phone and then continued on praying.

Two days later, in church on Sunday morning, a new worship song was introduced—one that carried incredible anointing. Sure enough, it had been written by the same musician I had observed 'getting a song' during the earlier prayer meeting. I realised that he had not written it because he had been searching for a song to write that day, but instead, a new song had *found* him because he was called, gifted and ready to receive it as a skilled songwriter and worship leader. Recognising the opportunity, perhaps in the form of some melodies or lyrics floating around in his head, he activated his skills and talents to create a song that would take our church to a brand new level of worship!

This musician was not searching for a song to write that day. The song that God had destined him to write FOUND him. It was drawn to the one who was created to write it. In fact, Scripture tells us that God is constantly searching for people who are committed to Him, so that He might display His strength in their lives.

> *For the eyes of the Lord range throughout the earth to strengthen those whose hearts are fully committed to him...*
>
> — *2 Chronicles 16:9 (NKJV)*

When God's strength is displayed in our lives, the outcome is far superior to anything we could ever achieve in our own human strength!

Without a shadow of a doubt, that beautiful song was not looking for me. Although I have been known to lead myself in worship in the shower, or bust out spontaneous renditions of Bohemian Rhapsody in our office corridors, my musical 'gift' will probably never translate to songs that can be sung by the masses. On the other hand, big ideas find me— usually in unexpected moments—because I have positioned myself in my own unique lane. Though I would love to have a songwriting gift that catapults a congregation to new levels of praise and worship, it is simply not God's purpose for my life. WHO I AM attracts the tasks that God has ordained for me alone to accomplish. My DOING flows naturally from my THINKING which is formed by my BEING.

Preparation = Readiness

In no small part, this young staff member's ability to readily receive and compose the Heaven-sent song was the result of years spent mastering his musical gift. Even if positioned to receive the song, he would have delayed its birth if he did not have the ability to wrap the correct musical chords around the lyrics. Being an excellent musician certainly played a role in calling down something of Heaven to Earth and the same is true in every endeavour of our lives that God has called us to. Positioning ourselves to receive ideas, resources, inspiration and strategies from God is one thing, but preparing our gifts and talents to see those things materialise and bear fruit, is another.

I wonder how many God-given opportunities remain untapped, waiting for us to hone our gifts and talents in preparation for stewarding those opportunities with excellence. What scientific breakthroughs, architectural masterpieces, solutions to poverty, cures for disease, breathtaking artworks, generationally impacting songs or technological advances await our readiness to receive them—according to our God-given purpose?

Maybe the answer is as simple as operating in our royal identity and committing ourselves to being life-long students—disciplined and determined to perfect and increase the raw ingredients God has gifted us.

> **The hand of the diligent will rule...**
> — *Proverbs 12:24 (NKJV)*

The Bible makes it clear that we have a responsibility to develop our own unique gifts and talents with excellence and diligence. In John 17:22, Jesus speaks of giving His followers the very same glory that the Father gave Him. This *glory* is why the Church can be the 'light of the world' and a 'city on a hill', shining with splendour and brightness (Matthew 5:14). But too often, believers miss opportunities to shine and to rule because we have not understood our identity or stewarded our gifts.

Not only do we attract creative ideas and strategies to our lives as we run in our own lane, but also resources. As we saw in the story of Nehemiah, the foreign king ended up providing all the protection and resources needed for the rebuilding of the wall. What remarkable favour!

When you chase your purpose, God will take care of the rest!

Nehemiah's fundraising opportunities did not come because he strived to make money. He merely ran in his lane and had the boldness to take hold of those opportunities when the moment arose. The moral of the story is this: you don't have to chase money because money is a natural byproduct of running in your purpose. When you chase your purpose, God will take care of the rest!

> **But seek first his kingdom and his righteousness, and all these things will be given to you as well.**
> — *Matthew 6:33 (NIV)*

As well as resources, living in our purpose as we steward our God-given gifts and talents also attracts something money cannot buy: *influence*.

Jamaican sprinter, Usain Bolt, is widely considered to be the greatest sprinter of all time. At the time of writing he holds the men's world 100 metre sprint record and, prior to his retirement, attracted the highest fee ever for an individual athlete in track and field, as Brand Ambassador for Pepsi. What I love about this champion is the fact that he spent his entire life perfecting his unique talent—sprinting—and became an influential voice in society because of his single-minded focus. Although he possibly had passing thoughts of one day being famous and influential, I'm sure as a young boy discovering that he was good at something, he simply focused on getting better at it. The incredible influence he now enjoys followed naturally.

The key question is this: Are you ready to receive the ideas, strategies, resources and influence that God has prepared for you as your kingly inheritance? Or are you too busy trying to get ahead in your human strength—working yourself into the ground, networking and diversifying—in search of those keys that will launch you to the next level? What if the Holy Spirit is right now trying to get your attention? Maybe all it will take to hear His voice (breathing creative ideas and urging you in exciting new directions) is dialing down the noise of the daily grind.

Timing is Everything

Sometimes we run ahead of God's purpose for our lives, gradually moving off course. My experience is that God moves slowly and will not bypass His own purpose in our lives just to keep up with us as we run aimlessly, hoping to stumble upon His favour and blessing. God is a God of *order*, and He has purpose in every step of our journey.

> ***Now I say that the heir, as long as he is a child, does not differ at all from a slave, though he is master of all, but is under guardians and stewards until the time appointed by the father.***
>
> *— Galatians 4:1-2 (NKJV)*

In the natural, a young prince has guardians or managers employed to train him in the duties and responsibilities of future kingship. Such training is meticulous, focussed and thorough in preparing him to rule and reign in a way that represents the values of the kingdom and of his family. Without it, a prince might succumb to the privilege of his existence and not manage the responsibility that comes with it. This in turn might place the entire kingdom over which he will one day rule in a position of vulnerability and distort the ancient culture on which it was built. As the scripture above says, even though the prince is an heir to the throne, he cannot take it until the father deems him ready to do so—and any good father knows that privilege and responsibility released too soon has the potential to corrupt the child and endanger the kingdom.

In much the same way, God's plan to shape and form us for rulership and dominion cannot be hurried or bypassed. The sooner we yield to Him, giving Him time and focus in our lives, the sooner we will be made ready to take the throne.

I finish this discussion by reminding us all that we were created with one purpose that is common to us all—to bring *glory* to God.

I have given them the glory that you gave me, that they may be one as we are one.
                                                        — John 17:22 (NIV)

That is the reason for our existence. Everything we do must have its focus on God's glory. When we get this revelation, we suddenly realise that we are not the same as every other businessperson or professional competing in the marketplace. We are different, set apart for a higher calling—the same tasks but a higher purpose.

When we choose to radically retrain our thinking and see ourselves as the kings God has called us to be—simplifying our lives, confronting our fears and trusting in the anointing that presides over our unique calling— and when we invest our resources into developing our relationship with God and refining our unique gifts and talents, then we will step into the new level of fruitfulness that we all desire. Heaven's supply line will open wide, delivering the ideas, resources and strategies that we need to rule over our assigned territory in the marketplace.

So are you ready to make a change? Don't just power on down the same path hoping for a different result. Many professionals I have known keep asking God to bless their endeavours but are unwilling to take the faith steps needed to reposition them for their divine purpose and inheritance. A supernatural result will require a spiritual strategy, but man-made strategies will accomplish man-made results. It's that simple.

Many are the plans in a person's heart, but it is the Lord's purpose that prevails.

— Proverbs 19:21 (NIV)

If you can grasp the full truth of your royal identity in Christ—allowing it to shape and form your thoughts and embolden you to break free of existing limitations—then you will begin to attract everything that you require to fulfil your God-given purpose on Earth.

Are you ready to accept the responsibilities of your kingship?

Your 'Red Box' awaits.

CHAPTER 4 DO

RUNNING TO WIN

*Brothers and sisters, I do not consider myself yet to
have taken hold of it. But one thing I do: Forgetting
what is behind and straining toward what is ahead, I
press on toward the goal to win the prize for which
God has called me heavenward in Christ Jesus.*

— Philippians 3:13-14 (NIV) —

Now that you have begun challenging some of the limiting mindsets in your life, it's time to look at the habits and disciplines that will help position you for holistic success and longevity as a king and priest in the ministry of business.

It is well known that kings-in-waiting are trained from a very young age for their role as a ruling monarch later in life. I recently read that Prince William's oldest son, Prince George—currently third in line to the English throne behind his father and grandfather—began training to be king from the age of five years old. This required him to sit with the current Queen of England for two hours per week to discuss what was expected of him as heir to the throne. I confess that this information came from a British tabloid so I have no idea whether or not it is true, but it makes sense that training for greatness must start as early as possible.

Preparing for the Race

Future kings are trained in a holistic way that covers every aspect of their lives and responsibilities so that they are ready to take the throne and uphold royal culture when their time comes. Their journey to the throne is a marathon and not a sprint. Given what is at stake, the purpose for their lives is outworked in a gradual, systematic way that cannot and should not be rushed.

When we have the mindset of a king, we are secure in the fact that we have a purpose that will be fulfilled in God's timing. As such, we too should keep the endgame in mind, approaching our training in a strategic way that is free from self-imposed pressure to get it all right all at once. I have learned first-hand that when I am trying to get healthy and lose weight, only slow and systematic changes in my behaviour that accompany changes in my thinking—though frustrating—actually lead to sustainable results and long-term success. The same is true in every area of my life.

The good news is that it doesn't matter where you find yourself today, there are skills and disciplines that you can learn in order to become all that you are called to be. In the next few chapters we will begin to investigate some of the most common skill sets that I believe distinguish those who excel in the marketplace from those who do not. However, it is important to remember that you don't need to be anxious about this or struggle to *make* yourself a person that God can use. You are ALREADY royalty in His eyes and He will journey WITH you, to draw OUT of you, what He placed IN you before you were born!

I ask you to consider putting in place habits that will bear long-term fruit—even if in the short-term, there may be no real evidence of their benefit. These habits have been gleaned from my own life and the lives of many business leaders who have proven their effectiveness first-hand.

Winning the Race

Do you not know that in a race all the runners run, but only one gets the prize? Run in such a way as to get the prize.

— 1 Corinthians 9:24 (NIV)

We are each called to run in a unique race that God has prepared for our lives and there is no doubt that He desires to see us succeed in finishing that race strong and enjoying the winner's rewards. Many of those ambitions and drives that constantly surface in our hearts,are not there by chance, but have been planted by God, along with the strength, gifts and talents, to see His will and calling fulfilled in our lives.

> *For it is [not your strength, but it is] God who is*
> *effectively at work in you, both to will and to work [that*
> *is, strengthening, energizing, and creating in you the*
> *longing and the ability to fulfil your purpose] for His good*
> *pleasure.*
>
> — *Philippians 2:13 (AMP)*

Although we are called to race and take our place at the starting line, it doesn't automatically mean that we will win or even finish that race— even when we are the only one competing for the prize that has been prepared specifically and uniquely for us.

One thing I have noticed in the years I have worked alongside business professionals is that too often they have a misconception of what it means to win their race. Very few who are called to marketplace ministry need to be coerced into racing. The motivation and drive to conquer and win are rarely in short supply. However, too many learn the hard way that unless their race is pre-planned, navigated with God-given wisdom and supported by Holy Spirit-assisted discipline, they may end up with a very different prize than the one they were created to win.

Jesus put it this way:

> *For what will it profit a man if he gains the whole world,*
> *and loses his own soul?*
>
> — *Mark 8:36 (NKJV)*

When applied to the context of business, this verse could read: What does it profit a businessperson to procure great wealth and success, but lose the things of greatest value—that can never be purchased with money—along the way?

I am aware that some of you reading this book may have already suffered losses while running your race, but the good news is that God's grace is sufficient to turn any challenging situation around. It just requires a little faith, repentance and obedience.

The Price of Success

The pursuit of marketplace success places huge demand on our limited time and resources, often stealing from those closest to us who legitimately have a claim to them in our lives. Juggling these resources to accommodate everyone's demands can be one of the greatest challenges in the life of a businessperson, and failure to manage this well can cause our lives to quickly spiral out of control.

I have often heard professionals justify the excessive attention they give to the pursuit of business, using the excuse that they are building a stable future for their families. While there is truth in the fact that wealth may bring a level of security in the long term, what good will that be if we have missed the formative years of our children's lives, neglected our marriages to the point of breakdown or lost our faith in God?

What's more, we cannot underestimate the effects that poor choices can have on our long-term health. We live in a world where stress, pressure and burnout are commonplace—even expected as part of the normal life of a businessperson. I was recently touring the beautiful offices of a very large and successful law firm in Melbourne, and noticed that they had a fully functioning first-aid room with a bed and medical intervention supplies. When I asked about the room, I was told that the law industry is an environment of chronic high stress and long work hours, and that the room was essential for the company to manage the resulting health conditions experienced by employees at work. I was shocked to think that stress-related illness would be so accepted and accommodated as the norm!

The marketplace is filled with too many 'successful' businesspeople with broken families and broken lives. But that does not need to be your story. When you have a revelation of your kingly identity, you understand that running to win is not about short-term success or monetary gain. It is about living out the fullness of your God-given purpose and thriving in every area of your life. Running to win is what you were born to do, but it requires great discipline, forward planning, experienced coaches and a consistent training regime.

Embracing Discipline

Discipline is one of those words that fills most of us with dread, but if we want to run the race of our lives well and finish strong, we must accept that there is no way around it.

Every king understands that with privilege comes responsibility. Despite the lavish lifestyle we observe when watching modern monarchs live out their lives on TV and social media, their unseen reality is far less glamorous and desirable. We imagine them sipping drinks by the pool, roaming from country to country on private jets and being pampered all day long in whatever way they desire—but often just the opposite is true. They belong to the people they serve and their life is not their own. They live highly disciplined and scheduled lives that revolve around the service of their people and we have seen how some will do anything they can to escape this so-called 'privilege' in search of a simpler and more private life.

Assuming your God-given identity as a king and priest in the marketplace demands discipline and sacrifice. Like Jesus, we have been called to a life of *service*. The more we understand our purpose and begin attracting the privilege and favour of Heaven, the greater responsibility we have to live our lives in a disciplined and accountable way. We must recognise that

Heaven's resources are released for the primary purpose of assisting us to govern wisely, uphold the culture of Heaven and extend the Kingdom of God—and NOT for our personal gain alone.

Dictators, on the other hand, often abandon all personal disciplines after taking their position of authority by force. Their impoverished mindset causes them to become self-indulgent and void of desire to genuinely serve the people they now govern. Examples of these kinds of people often hit our news when their lack of discipline is exposed. For example, consider high level executives earning huge salaries who forget that they were originally employed to serve people, and instead, line their own pockets while their customers suffer life-altering losses.

The Apostle Paul was an ordinary man who was dramatically converted to Christianity in an amazing encounter and called to advance the Kingdom of God. He would turn out to live a highly influential life with lasting eternal impact through his New Testament writings and many missionary endeavours. It is no surprise then that Paul understood the principle of discipline. After exhorting us to run in such as way as to win the prize (1 Corinthians 9:24), he elaborates on the attitude we must adopt in order to achieve this:

> *Therefore I do not run like someone running aimlessly; I do not fight like a boxer beating the air. No, I strike a blow to my body and make it my slave so that after I have preached to others, I myself will not be disqualified for the prize.*
>
> *— 1 Corinthians 9:26-27 (NIV)*

By referring to making his body his *slave*, he implies that we must be in control of our flesh and not vice versa. An alternate translation is, "I discipline my body and prepare it to serve." Paul is emphasising that in order to live a life that is fruitful and pleasing to God, self-control is vital.

Ask yourself the question: Am I in control of my life, or is something else? The issue of what or who is in control is one we will all wrestle with constantly in life, but we will never be empowered to correct any dysfunction until we dare to ask ourselves this question and answer it with humility and honesty. It can be very confronting but necessary to discover that you were never really in control at all!

There is often a great gap between intention and reality in our lives resulting in ongoing feelings of frustration and failure that weigh heavily on us. We intend to spend more time with our families, express more love to our spouses, commit more time to reading our Bibles and prayer, and to exercising regularly. However, we often fail to maintain the habits that we are trying to establish. After a certain number of failed attempts, most of us give up trying altogether and learn to accept failure in certain areas as our 'new normal'.

Galatians 5:22-23 tells us that self-control is a fruit of the Holy Spirit. Think about that for a moment. Self-control can mean nothing other than telling myself to do something that I don't want to do. So self control is not passive, but neither is it self-will. When I am running in my God-given purpose, I have the authority to command my flesh to do what it does not want to do and I have the promise that all of Heaven will back me up!

In other words, self-control is a work of the Holy Spirit in our lives. He gives us the power and ability to practise self-control so that we will not be mastered by the desires of our flesh that are always pulling us away from the purpose and plans of God.

This is especially relevant when we consider the unique temptations faced in the area of business. Think for a moment about physical appetite. God created a mechanism within us to inform us when our bodies are in need of nutrients to sustain activity. When our stomach rumbles, we become aware of our hunger and we eat. This is a healthy, God-designed process, but how quickly the same behaviour can wander into the 'sin zone' when we begin to ignore the signals and overindulge when we are not hungry. Our lack of self-discipline leads us away from the safety and wisdom of godly boundaries and into the place of self-destruction. The same is true in our working context. The once-godly desires to excel and succeed that were placed in our hearts for Kingdom purpose, can so easily turn into a relentless drive for more that causes our lives to spin off course and incur collateral damage in our relationships and health. That is why we must be people of self-discipline who seek the Holy Spirit's constant assistance in keeping within the boundaries that we (under His Lordship) set for our lives!

The concept of delayed gratification comes into play here. Most of us can recall moments when we were taught as children to delay gratification in our lives. I remember learning this principle when my parents would not let me eat dessert until I had finished my dinner. The gap between what I wanted and the task in front of me seemed so big, but there was no way around it. At times, I had to hold my nose in order to swallow the food I hated, while at other times, I carefully slipped it to the dog under the table. Incredibly, I always found a way to get the job done in order to win the *prize* of dessert. The same was true of completing my homework before being allowed to watch TV!

Somehow, in adulthood, we lose that knowledge and discipline that was built into our lives as children. Being an empowered adult allows us to decide for ourselves whether or not we will delay our gratification, and so often we slip back into the childishness of giving our flesh exactly what it wants when it wants it. Those who are called to marketplace ministry must understand that there will be times when we won't get what we want when we want it, because much more is at stake than satisfying our immediate cravings.

Most understand this in the context of business and career advancement. When we are young, fresh out of university or starting our first business, we understand that there are sacrifices to be made in the beginning for long-term gain. Often we must work very hard for minimal pay in order to advance and gain experience. Many professionals begin their journey as someone's assistant or apprentice, just to get a foot in the door and experience behind them. There is a cost to future success. This is a normal way of thinking in business, but how many of us are equally committed to putting disciplines in place to ensure that our families, relationships and health are also experiencing growth and success?

The truth is, living a life of self-discipline means enduring temporary discomfort for future gain.

The truth is, living a life of self-discipline means enduring temporary discomfort for future gain.

I have had to learn this in my own life. My job requires me to travel excessively, but I have learned to discipline myself in ways that maintain health in my family relationships. There are times when I choose to book 'nightmare flights' in order to make it home to attend functions that are important to my kids. At other times, when I arrive back to my hotel room—jet-lagged and exhausted from a gruelling day's work—I have trained myself to keep a small reserve of energy aside so that I can FaceTime my family so they feel like I am present in their lives. Neither of these choices come easily and both cost me something, but the *prize* of maintaining strong, healthy and intimate relationships with my family along life's journey is well worth it!

I love what is said of Jesus when faced with unimaginable suffering:

> *For the joy set before him he endured the cross, scorning its shame, and sat down at the right hand of the throne of God.*
>
> *— Hebrews 12:2 (NIV)*

He knew that the key to enduring immediate discomfort and winning His race was to maintaining resolute focus on the joy that lay ahead. What a powerful example He set for us all!

So what are you doing right now to invest in your future—in every area of your life? What disciplines are in place that are costing you precious time, money and energy? Are you holding loosely to the hope that one day you will enjoy peace with your kids, a rich and rewarding marriage, great health and intimacy with God, or are you acting now to ensure that those dreams will not remain fantasies?

When a king takes his throne, he is given enormous power to decide what is right for himself and for others. Few brave souls will question his indulgences, poor judgements, immoral choices or questionable time management, while he is wielding the sceptre. That is why it is crucial that kings are trained in personal discipline and accountability well before they are empowered to choose for themselves. The same is true of any one of us who desires to step into our God-given authority.

Advanced Decision Making

This day I call the heavens and the earth as witnesses against you that I have set before you life and death, blessings and curses. Now choose life, so that you and your children may live.

— Deuteronomy 30:19 (NIV)

One of the most incredible gifts God gives His children is the power and freedom to choose, but as we see in this scripture, He strongly urges us to choose *wisely*. Every decision we make in life has consequences attached, so it is important that we manage the gift of choice with wisdom.

Decisions that bring life into our circumstances are most powerful when made long before temptation presents itself. I call this 'Advanced Decision Making'. For example, choosing to set aside a non-negotiable date night with our spouse or partner is best made long before an 'opportunity of a lifetime' arises and demands our attention on that very

SCAN & WATCH

same night. Likewise, the decision to read our Bibles or take a walk each morning is best made long before we stay up late, working a deal or checking emails well into the small hours of the morning, or are invited to attend a last-minute breakfast with potential clients.

Decisions that bring life into our circumstances are most powerful when made long before temptation presents itself.

Of course I am not suggesting that there aren't times when we need to be flexible with our private lives or expect to be supported with understanding by our loved ones when unusual circumstances arise, but when these 'opportunities' become regular thieves of the time and energy we have promised to ourselves and others, the delicate rhythm we have been fighting for in our lives begins to falter. Even worse, when we actively look for opportunities to break our commitment to things we don't particularly enjoy and call it 'opportunity', we know we are in trouble!

Self-control is all about engaging overriding responses. It's about shutting down those desires or temptations that crop up as we go through life, threatening to steal the prize. The best way to shut them down is to DECIDE, in advance, what course of action we intend to take—no matter what circumstances present themselves in the moment.

Running our race in such a way as to win begins with establishing a clear vision for every area of our lives and then making decisions that will lead us to the fulfilment of that vision. When these decisions have been made in advance and settled in our hearts, and the inevitable moments of distraction or temptation arise, we will not need to depend on sheer willpower to stay on course. Our natural willpower is a weak and unpredictable resource that cannot be relied on in times of pressure or opportunity. According to cognitive neuroscientists, well thought out decisions, on the other hand, are robust pathways in our brain that will lead us towards, and not away from, the end goal. In other words, our brain is less likely to resist doing what is right but difficult, if we have already forged a decision pathway.

Just like brushing our teeth, we must make the important life decisions that relate to our health, our family, our marriages, our friendships, our finance and most of all, our relationship with God—automatic and instinctive.

So I don't know what that means for you personally in the context of your life, but I have put this principle into practice strategically over my lifetime—knowing that I am prone to being a workaholic by nature. Some of the many decisions I have made in advance include establishing set working hours and turning off from work when walking into my home; giving to my church via direct debit to ensure I am not affected by my financial circumstances at the time; establishing a 'date day' with my wife that is non-negotiable and work-free; where possible, never booking travel when my family have birthdays and always being available to transport my teenage children to local church youth programs.

On that note, I made a decision long before my children were even a twinkle in my eye that we would be a family that serves the Lord and faithfully attends our local church. After choosing Jesus as my Lord and Saviour, this was the most important 'Advanced Decision' that I ever made and one I will NEVER regret— despite the inconveniences and personal costs incurred as a result!

Although the spotlight is on our private lives right now, applying Advanced Decision Making to your working practices will also yield great rewards. Deciding in advance how you will approach spending, staying focussed on core business, ongoing training and building relationships with your team—just to name a few areas—will protect you from neglecting these important areas when distractions, busyness, stress and temptations try to lure you away from the goal.

So what is your vision for your personal life—health, relationships and spirituality? Do you have the same clarity with these as you do your career? What 'advanced decisions' need to be made to protect the delicate balance of your life and to help you run in such a way as to win?

If you need further inspiration, look to the example set by Jesus who decided to obey His Father's leading no matter what the cost, long before He began the gruelling journey to the cross. Yes, He had a temporary moment of anguish in Gethsemane where He pleaded with His Father to release Him from the commitment He had already made. But ultimately, nothing would deter Him from walking the path He had chosen long before. He is the ultimate example of 'Advanced Decision Making' and its power to lead you to the finish line with great strength and dignity, even in the most challenging of circumstances imaginable!

Check the Foundations

As I have mentioned, prior to stepping into full-time ministry, I was a commercial builder by trade. One of the most fascinating processes I learned prior to leaving the industry was the process of laying *foundations*. For many months, no progress could be seen on the build from the street level which left people frustrated and impatient—especially investors. This was the time when huge earthworks were taking place that would allow the building above to be securely anchored into the bedrock. The company would manage the impatience of the people by erecting an artist's impression of the completed building at street level, so they would be reminded of what would be when the slow process of building foundations was complete.

The time taken and depth of the foundations needed was directly proportional to the magnitude of the building above, so the bigger the build, the longer the foundations would take to prepare. Any attempt to speed up the process and cut corners in order to respond to the demands of people would risk constructing something that was unsafe in the long-term—but this was difficult for most people to understand.

Strong foundations are not a new concept. Jesus Himself used the analogy of building a house on sand versus rock (see Matthew 7:24-27) and the long-term implications of making a hasty, convenient decision that seemed right in the moment. The short-term gain and satisfaction of building a house quickly and effortlessly was overshadowed by the disaster of losing that house as soon as life brought unexpected resistance. The parable ends with the tragic words, "...and great was its fall". Jesus was pointing to the importance of firm foundations in our lives, something we so often neglect to invest time into in our quest to build something significant—even when our heart is to build it for Him!

I love that God showed me this process in the natural many years ago and spoke to me about the importance of foundations in our lives. Have you recently inspected the foundations of your marriage, parenting, health, friendships, finance and relationship with God? When was the last time you checked whether there were any cracks? Have you been so busy pushing forward that you neglected to build strength into them? Are your dreams for your family or business far greater than the foundations you have built can bear? Take my advice; quick and easy success rarely leads to anything that lasts the test of time and resistance. Rapid success comes at a great cost—you may not have to pay it immediately, but make no mistake, you will be required to settle the account one day and it may cost you everything.

The truth is, we will never notice the cracks that are forming in our foundations, the danger of cliff-edge that we are precariously balancing on, or the little foxes that are relentlessly munching on our vines if we do not invest time into our busy lives for reflection and prayer—two disciplines that so easily fall to the bottom of the priority list in the life of the business person.

Pacing Yourself

Constantly throwing everything we have—time, money, energy and attention—into the 'now opportunity' without adequately considering and preparing for the long-term *prize*, can have devastating effects in our lives.

One of the greatest temptations we all face is to seek the affirmation of people or the 'high' of a great conquest in the moment, while losing focus on the long-term God-dream. We are constantly being scrutinised and either celebrated or criticised for our current performance, so it is easy to treat each daily challenge with the same, or even greater, importance as the end game. In doing this, we often neglect the daily disciplines required to run the race well and finish strong.

The truth is, the race we are running to win is not a sprint, but a marathon.

The truth is, the race we are running to win is not a sprint, but a marathon, and every marathon runner understands the importance of pacing themself.

I recently read an account by a rookie marathon runner who learned this the hard way. As the young man bolted off from the starting blocks of his first-ever marathon, he maintained a fast pace up to the 24km mark feeling invincible! That's where everything changed—suddenly and catastrophically!

He recalls that after the euphoria of the 'runner's high' began to settle, he started feeling light headed and his legs began to fail. Within a small space of time, he began to wonder if he would even be able to finish the race, let alone win. He describes this moment as 'hitting a wall.' This first-timer had approached the marathon race like a sprinter and paid the price accordingly.

Running marathons requires planning and strategy, and carefully sticking to that plan during the race when your mind and body are urging you to deviate from it for temporary gain. This discipline of pacing ourselves is a concept that is generally foreign to the nature of ambitious and driven professionals. It means letting go of some of the temporary gains and opportunities for the sake of the real *prize* that stands at the end of our race. This is easier said than done and can only be truly embraced by those who are secure enough in their kingly identity and mature enough in their character development to trust God.

Let's think about the diet industry for a moment. It is very clear to us all that rapid, significant weight loss results rarely, if ever, translate to long-term, sustainable change. Yet many continue to seek out the 'quick fix' and to live on the immediate but transitory highs of success in the moment. Unfortunately, it is human nature to concentrate our energies on the 'here and now' and lose sight of the end game, but this cannot be our mindset if we want to be businesspeople who run our race 'in such a way as to win'. We must learn to *pace* ourselves.

Jesus Himself was the ultimate example of what it means to pace ourselves in life.

And Jesus grew in wisdom and stature, and in favor with God and man.

— *Luke 2:52 (NIV)*

For 30 years, He progressively matured and developed physically, relationally and spiritually, laying low until the time was right for Him to step into the spotlight and finish His race in the public eye. He was never in a hurry to move faster or beyond the place where His Father led Him. Even when His ministry life really began to find momentum, He never allowed the overwhelming demands to steer Him off course. He in turn, taught His disciples to do the same:

The apostles gathered around Jesus and reported to him all they had done and taught. Then, because so many people were coming and going that they did not even have a chance to eat, he said to them, "Come with me by yourselves to a quiet place and get some rest." So they went away by themselves in a boat to a solitary place.

— *Mark 6:30-32 (NIV)*

Even though He must have been so happy to see them busy and productive in their quest to build His Father's Kingdom, He advised them to pace themselves, knowing that they would not be able maintain this momentum as they grew more and more tired and depleted.

My dad used to advise me often, "Don't make any decisions when you are tired, angry or frustrated". This was great advice, but easier said than done when tiredness has become the norm in our lives! No matter how much we love God and the people in our lives, and want to live lives of integrity, we have all found ourselves teetering on the moral edge when the pressure is high and we are physically and emotionally drained. In these moments, we entertain thoughts of crossing lines that we would never normally cross because our vision is blurred. This is the 'danger zone' and the consequences of the poor decisions that result can linger around our lives for years, even causing us to quit the race short of winning the prize. The moral of the story is that we must never think that we are exempt from the trouble that accompanies self-imposed physical, mental or emotional exhaustion!

Jesus saw the urgent needs of the people for healing, deliverance and teaching. He was moved with compassion and compelled to reach out to them when they cried out to Him for help, but He understood the physical limitations of His humanity and knew when it was time to stop, rest and replenish. He imposed boundaries on His time so that He could focus on the things that He was PURPOSED to do.

Jesus understood the truth that every marketplace minister must settle in his or her heart. Many have told me over the years that they work hard in order to earn some rest and play at a later time (or they work themselves into the ground until they have no option but to rest). In other words, they work in order to rest. Work is seen as the *price* to be paid for the *prize* of rest. This thinking is out of order! Jesus rested in order that He could work more effectively.

If we fail to be intentional about rest, we should not be surprised that God may at times stand in our way and force the issue. When this happens, it can seem as though we are being punished or the enemy is at work limiting our momentum. But sometimes this is the act of a loving Father who understands that exhaustion makes us more vulnerable to temptation, conflict and poor decision-making. Ultimately, He uses these frustrating moments in our lives not just to slow us down and protect us from ourselves, but also to alter our perspective in ways that enlarge us on the inside.

Real rest has a way of adjusting our perspective and regaining godly balance in our lives when we assign value and gratitude to it.

I heard it said once that you don't burn out because of what you DO, but because of what you FAIL TO DO. Neglecting the essential areas of our lives will inevitably lead us to a place where we are too spent and depleted to do anything of value at all!

I, like most of you, love the thrill of the chase and the high that living a busy, action-packed life offers us. Years ago, when visiting Tokyo, Japan, I found myself swallowed up in a sea of people rushing from here to there, busy going about their normal lives. I had never seen such activity and I loved it! I was told that 25-30 million people lived within a radius of 20 km and the effect was a kind of controlled mayhem that gave me a real buzz! There were moments when the momentum of the crowd was so strong that I was caught up in the motion and literally couldn't turn around and walk in the other direction!

While I enjoyed the novelty of this for a while, I soon needed to escape the chaos and took a lift up to a lounge on the 39th floor of a nearby hotel. There was a band playing quietly and the ambience was relaxing and calm when I arrived and looked down on the chaos from the peaceful heights above. I was in the very same location, but at a higher altitude, and everything had changed. My perspective had changed and as a result, the natural stress and demands of the crowds below fell away. After some time, I felt refreshed, ready and eager to get back amongst it!

This is why it is so important that we actively build in moments of reflection and rest into our lives. These are not benefits to be enjoyed when time permits, but are essential to our ability to run our race with strength and endurance. When the chaotic circumstances of our lives are viewed from a position of rest, a new perspective comes, and the road forward emerges with clarity and conviction.

When the chaotic circumstances of our lives are viewed from a position of rest, the road forward emerges with clarity and conviction.

Are you pacing yourself for the race?

Enjoy the Ride!

The thief comes only to steal and kill and destroy; I have come that they may have life, and have it to the full.
— *John 10:10 (NIV)*

Read this passage of scripture too quickly and you may miss the message Jesus is trying to convey. He did not come to give us a full life, but instead, life to the full. There is a big difference!

I want to finish our discussion about running our race well by looking for a moment at the subject of *enjoyment*.

Though most businesspeople I know would report that they enjoy their work, most would also admit that at times, it leaves them depleted of energy, peace and joy. What defines true recreation is its ability to replenish us in these areas and restore us to functioning at our full potential. What restores each one of us is as uniquely different as we are. What I love to do for fun, others may find pure torture!

Sadly, recreation can be viewed as an unnecessary luxury for the time-challenged or work-driven, but it is so important if we want to finish our race strong. I have already confessed that I am as driven and ambitious as the next man when it comes to my profession, but I have learned that really special moments await you when you stop and engage in activities outside of work.

I remember visiting the beautiful Lake District in England with my wife shortly before we started having children. We didn't have a lot of money to spend, but decided to save up, plan and take a budget holiday to escape our busy lives. Even then, I was aware that hairline cracks were forming in the foundations of my marriage—as the stresses and pressure of our lifestyle began to take their toll—so I thought it best to get away and reconnect.

My wife loves all things 'nature' and I chose the scenic location for her benefit. To my surprise, I was unexpectedly impacted myself!

I remember walking hand-in-hand along the edge of a glistening lake, listening to the sound of a Dixieland Jazz band playing in the distance. It was as if life stood still for a moment to let us off the treadmill. It honestly felt like I was in Heaven as the restoration of my spirit and body began to take effect. But like most of these moments in life, the bliss was so quickly forgotten when I returned to work and the treadmill started up at full pace once again.

When our children were born, we began to dream about a future where they would come and bring their own families on holiday with us— hopefully when we were more cashed-up! It was a dream in our hearts that would never happen without us creating a plan, so we decided to set aside 2-3 weeks every two years to take a significant holiday with our children. We wanted to expose them to as many parts of the world as possible so they could return to their favourite places as adults to explore them further.

From the time Kimberley and Ryan were toddlers, we put our vision into action, planning and saving up for our holidays. As our wealth increased, so too did the quality of these holidays.

I can honestly say that these vacations turned out to be *game-changers* for our family, creating life-long memories and bonding us together strongly in ways that everyday routine could not. It wasn't always convenient from a time and finance perspective, and it often took a huge amount of self-control for me to switch off my mind and my phone to be present in the moment. But now I am the greatest advocate of replenishing rest with those that you love. I honestly don't know how I or my family could have survived the hectic pace of the last 20 years of our lives without these regular and intentional *time outs* along the way.

Part of God's design for us is that we would *enjoy* life (1 Tim 6:17) by remaining connected with Him and surrounded by meaningful relationships, enjoying the wonders of His creation and partnering with Him to see His Kingdom come on Earth. You should never feel guilty for stealing a little time (and finance) for yourself and your family. You should thoroughly *relish* time spent lounging by the pool, laughing with a friend as you drive down the golf course, swinging your legs over the side of a boat—wind in the hair—munching on choc tops and popcorn at the movies, snoring in the day spa or attacking the buffet on a cruise ship. These moments in time are a *gift* and essential if we are to steward the ONE life we have been given, as well as the lives of those we partner with and those we bring into the world.

Just as Jesus intentionally took time for rest so that He could be more effective in His ministry, so too will your work be waiting for you on the other side of a few moments of stillness and serenity. But if you are a driven person like me, it will take self-control, advance decision making and intentionality to take time out to rest and be restored.

Like many professionals and business owners I have encountered over my lifetime, please don't lean on the excuse that you are just in a 'building phase' of life that won't last forever—thereby robbing yourself and your family of moments of true refreshing that may not come again. I have found that so many of these men and women are still building 30 years later, while living lonely, disconnected and exhausting lives and blindly chasing a dream for the future that never comes.

So what is it all for anyway? What is the end goal of your life right now?

Are you enjoying your life? Is there room for doing what you love with the people that you love?

Ready or not, the race has already begun. Even in your wildest dreams, you could not imagine what God has already planned for you—not only at the end of your race, but all along the way.

We have all heard it said so many times that the journey is more important than the destination, but I think they are both as important as each other. Getting the best out of the race is going to mean taking the time out to plan and prepare yourself so you will run it well, complete it and take out the prize.

> *I have fought the good fight, I have finished the race, I have kept the faith.*
> *— 2 Timothy 4:7 (NIV)*

SCAN & WATCH

So stop wishing things were better and just do it!

Choose LIFE. I dare you.

THE POWER
OF FOCUS

"If you chase two rabbits, you won't catch either one."

— Russian Proverb —

The human eye is one of the most incredible of God's creations and one He loves to use as an analogy for all sorts of principles. The process of seeing is very complex, but I will attempt to explain it as simply as I can for the purpose of applying its lessons to our lives as ministers in the marketplace.

Light is emitted from the sun or a man-made source, sending out light beams that bounce off the objects around us before entering our eye through our pupil. The pupil then directs those beams through our lens, which in turn bends the light beams so that they hit the back of the eye (retina) in the exact position where the information can be sent to the brain to be interpreted.

This process of directing different light signals so that they can best be interpreted is called 'focussing' and the role of the lens in this process is crucial.

When the lens in our eye isn't working well, our brain is unable to interpret the information that is flooding into our eyes. While we can still see, the images are unclear causing our decisions and actions to be influenced by compromised information. It isn't that objects change their shape or location, but our ability to focus on and make sense of them is determined by the lens we are looking through. This is why it is crucial that we are looking at our lives through a healthy *lens*.

> *The eye is the lamp of the body. If your eyes are healthy, your whole body will be full of light. But if your eyes are unhealthy, your whole body will be full of darkness. If then the light within you is darkness, how great is that darkness!*
> — *Matthew 6:22-23 (NIV)*

When we see things clearly, we make more informed choices.

I think this analogy of the eye tells us so much about our lives and the crucial role that our ability to correctly focus plays. Where there is no clear focus—vision, perspective and movement are hindered. In some cases, the inability to focus all but blinds us and we are forced to navigate life, family, health, church and business with the same risk as a visually impaired person faces when navigating the natural world around them.

> *Where there is no vision, the people are unrestrained.*
> *— Proverbs 29:18 (NASB)*

If we are going to navigate our personal and business lives effectively and avoid pitfalls, what is the healthy lens through which we should view and evaluate life's decisions?

I believe that there are two crucial lenses that will help keep us focussed on our God-given destiny.

The first of these powerful lenses is **PURPOSE**.

The Lens of PURPOSE

When we live with a sense of clear purpose that flows from a secure identity as heirs of God's Kingdom on Earth, it becomes far easier to filter incoming information and remain focussed on what is crucial to our unique mandate. As we have discussed, we will never have clarity of purpose until we have clarity of identity.

The thoughts that emanate from a secure sense of identity help to refine and sharpen our God-given purpose and in turn, our day-to-day focus in decision-making.

We will never have clarity of purpose until we have clarity of identity.

Not that I have already obtained all this, or have already arrived at my goal, but I press on to take hold of that for which Christ Jesus took hold of me. Brothers and sisters, I do not consider myself yet to have taken hold of it. But one thing I do: Forgetting what is behind and straining toward what is ahead, I press on toward the goal to win the prize for which God has called me heavenward in Christ Jesus.

— Philippians 3:12-14 (NIV)

One of the most common issues I have found amongst marketplace professionals is the inability to focus on what is important to their calling and purpose. This is because the lens they are looking through is distorting their perspective. Instead of creating clear vision, the lens blurs their vision. I'm sure you've experienced this when you put on someone else's eye glasses. Your vision immediately becomes distorted and is disorienting because the lens was designed for their eyes and not yours.

If we are to function as kings in the marketplace, we must learn to use our sense of purpose to filter incoming information. This allows us to focus on what is critical to our mandate. Where there is no clarity of purpose, we will struggle to focus and be vulnerable to falling into the trap of chasing random opportunities and ideas.

When a king is secure in his identity and purpose, he is free to focus on the things that he alone is mandated to do. He does not react to the urgent demands that others place on him, but instead remains focussed on those things that are integral to his purpose. Layers of people are positioned to filter the incoming demands and assign them to appropriate others, allowing the king to elevate his vision to issues that have significant long-term repercussions for his kingdom and the subjects over which he rules. As we discussed previously, it is his *thinking* rather than his *doing* that keeps his kingdom secure and prosperous.

This kind of focussed thinking takes discipline, even for kings, as it is often necessary to outsource tasks that are enjoyable and rewarding to create space to focus on those that are most important.

We see this principle at work in the life of an eagle. Eagles have eyes that occupy over 50% of their head mass, giving them the sharpest vision of any animal and vastly superior to that of humans. Their ability to focus on something tiny from a large distance away is their super-power and what earns them the title of Apex Predator and King of the Birds! There are many lessons we can learn from them in our quest to be kings in the marketplace.

When an eagle takes off in flight, they head upwards, unconcerned about any potential threats that lie beneath them at a lower altitude. Instead, they focus on where they are headed, gliding effortlessly at high altitude.

While all other birds seek refuge on the ground from storms, the eagle uses the thermal winds that the storm creates to glide above it without needing to flap or work its wings. It is only when it is seeking prey that it looks down and locks in its focus. Interestingly, once they fix their gaze on an animal (being able to see a rabbit from 3.2km away), they never look away—regardless of any obstacles they face on their descent.

The high altitude that eagles operate in gives them a unique perspective on what is going on below and makes them a formidable and undetectable predator. In the same way, when we release 'ground level' responsibilities to others and choose instead to view our lives and businesses from a higher altitude, we make the most of our most valuable resource—our thinking.

When we choose to view our lives and and businesses from a higher altitude, we make the most of our most valuable resource—our thinking.

Are you clear about your purpose? Are you able to discern the difference between what is urgent and what is important on a daily basis? Do you spend the majority of your time at an altitude that enables you to see what is going on with focussed perspective or are you prone to chasing your tail around responding to the urgent demands that are placed at your feet daily?

Maybe it's time to view your life through the healthy lens of PURPOSE, asking yourself this one important question: Does this opportunity, idea or task fit within the scope of my PURPOSE?

If not, let it go.

The Lens of CAUSE

The second vital lens through which to view your life is CAUSE.

Built into the DNA of every human being is the desire to live for a great cause. It gives our lives the purpose and fulfilment that chasing success alone will never do. A great cause is a POWERFUL motivator that should not be underestimated.

Kings live with a strong sense of cause that guides them throughout their lives. Their cause is to see to it that their kingdom and their subjects live secure, healthy and prosperous lives. Their cause is not about themselves but the good of those whom they serve, and everything they do is sifted and interpreted through this lens.

Without a clear sense of cause, we often feel pulled between areas of our lives like a never-ending game of tug-of-war.

Without a clear sense of cause, we often feel pulled between areas of our lives like a never-ending game of tug-of-war. It can seem like just when we are kicking goals at work, our families are unhappy and demanding. Then, when things come together on the family front, work seems to fall apart. This lack of clarity and focus is tiring and we cope by *compartmentalising* our lives—shifting focus to the place it is needed at any given time.

How often I see professionals stop attending church when they are under pressure. I have personally spoken to many who after an intensely productive and demanding season at work, finally turn their attention to their neglected family and find them apathetic or disinterested in spending time with them. Some drop their exercising regime or sacrifice sleep and recreation when work pressure escalates, and are suddenly sidelined with chronic illness. Sadly, it is next to impossible to please everyone when you live with a 'compartment mindset', and our vision ends up blurred and confused.

The alternative is to view every area of our lives through the lens of *cause* and make our decisions according to the clarity of vision it brings. In essence, we must simplify our lives to live by one defining, singular, common cause, and that is, to partner with God to see cities and souls won and His Kingdom established—in both our working AND private lives.

> **For the Son of Man came to seek and to save the lost.**
> *— Luke 19:10 (NIV)*

When God's singular focus becomes our singular focus, all of the areas of our lives begin to align. Suddenly, we ALL become ministers, pursuing ONE vision alone regardless of our occupation. Standing in agreement with a greater cause than our own does not mean that we must abandon the pursuit of our unique purpose. It simply means that our purpose finds expression within the boundaries of that cause.

When God's singular focus becomes our singular focus, all of the areas of our lives begin to align.

I am reminded of my own journey into the ministry. In dedicating myself as a young man to the greatest cause there is—the Cause of Christ—and then viewing every part of my life through the lens of that Cause, God began to order my steps straight into my destiny. With each year that went by, my purpose became clearer and clearer. Each time something significant was added to my life—marriage, parenting, business—I kept viewing my daily decisions through the lens of the Cause, and the people around me followed suit. I can say with all humility that from a family perspective, the Cause of Christ has remained the single common thread that keeps us aligned, unified and blessed!

From the outside looking in, limiting my vision to the boundaries of the Cause of Christ may have looked like a great sacrifice that would limit my future potential, but that couldn't be further from the truth. My hopes and dreams found expression in ways that I could only have dreamed of and I discovered that those perceived boundaries were in fact springboards into even greater possibilities!

If we remember that we are kings, we will live lives that are cause-driven in every area—our family life; our church life; our investments; our influence; our ethics and morality; and our partnerships with others.

Viewing FAMILY
Through the Lens of Cause

My wife and I have worked in the ministry for most of our married life. We share a deep commitment to the Cause that has helped us to navigate life's natural challenges hand-in-hand. As in any business, there have been moments when the demands of our calling have placed stress on our family. Long, unconventional hours, being on call 24/7 and investing a lot of our income back into the church have all threatened to steal precious time, energy and resources from our children and at times, our marriage. But because we settled in our hearts a long time ago that the Cause of Christ would be central to our lives and that God would be faithful to provide for all of our needs, we rarely, if ever, pulled back in fear.

By looking through the lens of cause, we have been able to navigate the huge demands of ministry with unusual clarity and peace. Had we not had a common cause to bring order and focus, arguments over time spent at work versus home would have broken out constantly as each juggling ball in our life continually fought for our undivided attention and limited resources!

The same is true in the reverse. When our children are going through something challenging or our spouse needs special attention, neither of us hesitate to be there, even if it means sometimes delaying urgent work. Why? Because a strong, unified family is part of the Cause for which Jesus came to Earth, and stewarding them well pleases God. Both serving the church and serving our family are essential elements of the Cause which has enabled us to view our lives with flexibility, godly wisdom and responsiveness to the prompting of the Holy Spirit. This would simply not be possible if we saw work and home as two unrelated *compartments* of our lives.

A result of this is that our children have grown up to be equally dedicated to the Cause around which our lives have orbited as a family since their childhood.

Losing our children to the world or allowing our marriages to grow distant does nothing to glorify God or promote His Cause. No matter how honourable your intentions are in building a better financial future for your family or providing a better quality of life for your spouse, neglecting the essential elements of the Cause to achieve it is never acceptable. Every decision made must be viewed through the common lens of the

Cause so that every member of the family stands together, facing the same direction and focussed on the same corporate vision. We can do this confidently knowing that God will take care of the rest!

> *But seek first the kingdom of God and His righteousness,*
> *and all these things shall be added to you.*
> — *Matthew 6:33 (NKJV)*

When presented with the next idea or opportunity, ask yourself this question: Does this facilitate the Cause of Christ being outworked through my life?

If not, let it go.

Viewing CHURCH
Through the Lens of Cause

Why do you attend church? Is it simply another compartment of your life or juggling ball that you are working hard to keep in the air? If church is just an obligation for you or you secretly view it as a waste of precious time, it is destined to fall by the wayside as soon as another opportunity presents itself. These kinds of feelings should act as a red flag, urging you to re-evaluate the condition of your heart.

One of the things I hate the most is watching marketplace leaders neglect their relationship with God and eventually drift away from their churches, only to end up *shipwrecked* and in desperate need of God and the Church later in life. The simple truth is that the demands of business will always increase and present all kinds of reasons to draw you away from your faith, if you allow them to.

The decision to neglect attending your local church regularly is a decision to turn your back on the cause.

The Church is God's vehicle for revival on Earth and is central to the Cause. The decision to neglect attending your local church regularly, or relegating church to a lower priority status than it should be, is a decision to turn your back on the cause and lose your focus on the primary thing we have all been called to build.

> *And let us consider how we may spur one another on toward love and good deeds, not giving up meeting together, as some are in the habit of doing, but encouraging one another—and all the more as you see the Day approaching.*
>
> *— Hebrews 10:24-25 (NIV)*

One of the keys to staying focussed on and passionate about attending your local church is feeling a sense of ownership of the vision. Just as in business, we do not tend to prioritise things that we are not responsible for. After all, we have enough pressure already without worrying about the responsibilities of others. This is why it is so important to feel personal ownership of your church's vision so that you do not easily delegate or abdicate that responsibility to others when business opportunities present themselves.

When faced with your next decision or opportunity, ask yourself this: How will this affect my commitment to and service in my local church?

If it will be weakened, let it go.

Viewing INVESTMENT Through the Lens of Cause

Many businesspeople I know are constantly looking for opportunities to invest in order to build personal wealth and future security. Houses and property are some of the more common investments I see pursued in the driving quest to build a portfolio that protects hard-earned wealth against future challenging circumstances. Investment opportunities in business are more diverse and often carry far greater risk.

The truth is, the greater the risk, the greater our need for godly wisdom to make sound decisions that benefit and not disadvantage our lives.

We know from Scripture that God is an investor Himself (think of the parable of the talents), so the desire in us to invest and increase is simply a reflection of our Father's character in us. However, like anything, a legitimate pursuit can become an obsession.

Once again, the lens through which you view investments is very important. Often the benefits of making money (even very large amounts) are outweighed by the cost to other areas of our lives—our health, family, marriage and core business. However, when the same opportunity is viewed through the lens of the cause, our focus becomes clear and sharp, and we are positioned to make wise and profitable decisions that do not threaten the health and wellbeing of any area of our lives.

Looking for opportunities to invest is a wise, honourable and godly pursuit. What needs to be viewed through the lens of the Cause is our motivation for investing—what lies at the root of our endeavours and exploits. This can only be revealed as we dare to prayerfully ask some confronting questions:

Does this investment opportunity further the Cause of Christ or lead me away from it?

Will it help build the Kingdom of God or just my own kingdom?

Does it represent my own desires or God's?

Based on your honest responses to these questions, is it really worth it and part of God's plan for your life, family and business? Will God be in favour of it and bless it?

Viewing INFLUENCE Through the Lens of Cause

Influence is powerful but challenging thing to manage.

The pursuit of influence is a noble thing. Having Christian men and women sitting in positions of influence is invaluable in our mission to establish the Kingdom of God on Earth.

The Bible is full of examples of people who used their hard-earned influence at critical moments to see the Cause of Christ fulfilled. Consider Esther—a beautiful young girl who captured the heart of a king and was able to change the course of history when her 'for such a time as this moment' presented. She found herself in a position of influence at the right time and in the right place, and she seized an opportunity that paid huge dividends!

However, influence, when viewed through the wrong lens, has the ability to corrupt us and distort the vision we have for our lives. Unfortunately, far too many pastors and businesspeople alike have soared quickly to great heights of influence, only to discover the hard way that they did not have an adequate accountability structure around them to keep them focussed and on course to their destiny. They simply did not view their growing influence through the lens of the Cause and actually did damage to the Cause in the process. Still others drop the ball of family to throw themselves wholly into the pursuit of influence only to discover that the price of that influence was much higher than they wanted to pay!

With influence comes the responsibility to make decisions that impact many, so it is so important to process all such decisions through the lens of the Cause. As opportunities to grow in influence arise, ask yourself this question:

Is this influence consistent with the Cause of Christ?

Viewing MORALITY
Through the Lens of Cause

Too often, I am asked by businesspeople whether or not it is okay to cross the fine line of morality if the potential outcome will be profitable for their local church.

Very sad.

If businesspeople were looking through the lens of the Cause, then attractive but 'dodgy' opportunities would be clearly seen for what they are. Obviously, no opportunity that requires us to violate the Kingdom cultures of honesty and integrity has been sent by God for their good!

> *The integrity of the upright guides them, but the unfaithful are destroyed by their duplicity.*
> — *Proverbs 11:3 (NIV)*

The word 'duplicity' used in this proverb means 'perverseness and crooked dealing', and we are warned that this kind of behaviour will destroy those who deal in it. The word 'destroy' here means 'to utterly ruin, devastate, spoil and destroy'. You can't get a clearer message than that!

Breaking the law or breaching your integrity on any front not only provides a foothold for the enemy to advance, but undermines the culture and standards of the Kingdom of God. No matter how noble the intentions are for the potential profits, choosing to breach integrity moves us outside of the flow of God's blessing and favour. He will not ultimately bless what has been acquired by dishonest gain. Making a lifestyle of these compromises distorts our vision and leads us away from our destiny.

I am sad to say that so many businesspeople have admitted to me over the years that they deliberately cross lines into grey areas with an "I'll repent later for it" mentality. Really, they are just revealing spiritual immaturity that if not corrected, will catch up with them and keep them from operating in their God-given destiny.

> *Do not be deceived: God cannot be mocked. A man reaps what he sows.*
> — *Galatians 6:7 (NIV)*

When you look at an opportunity through the lens of the Cause, it is difficult to conclude that dodgy dealings are justifiable. Sometimes all we need to do is close the door. Many have looked to me as their pastor to help them close doors that they are struggling to close themselves due to the temptation of opportunity. They already know what I will say, but are hoping against hope that I will agree that the end is worth the means.

I never do.

Integrity is something to be protected and upheld. It will lead to places of influence and attract the Presence and favour of God.

Integrity is something to be protected and upheld.

> *Because of my integrity you uphold me and set me in your presence forever.*
> — *Psalm 41:12 (NIV)*

Credibility is challenging—though not impossible—to rebuild once damaged and is one of the most powerful ways that we can reflect the nature of our God to the corrupted world around us.

> *Do your best to present yourself to God as one approved, a worker who does not need to be ashamed and who correctly handles the word of truth.*
> — *2 Timothy 2:15 (NIV)*

It's time to close those doors. Stop wasting time dwelling on it. You already know the answer. Walk away if you want to walk in blessing.

When faced with a questionable opportunity or decision, ask yourself: Does this violate Kingdom culture and compromise my integrity as a king?

It it does, let it go.

Viewing PARTNERSHIP Through the Lens of Cause

Partnerships can greatly enhance the profitability of your business in the marketplace. However, not all partnerships will benefit your life and support the Cause.

I have witnessed the results of both beneficial and destructive partnerships in the life of businesspeople. While the good kind free us up and decrease our load, others do the very opposite. Some ultimately weigh down the business and our lives personally.

Most partnerships that do not succeed were destined to fail because the partners were unequally yoked.

Do not be yoked together with unbelievers. For what do righteousness and wickedness have in common? Or what fellowship can light have with darkness?
— *2 Corinthians 6:14 (NIV)*

A yoke is a wooden bar that was used to strap two oxen together at the neck to help them share the burden of pulling the plough. When one ox was taller or stronger than the other, they were unable to find the rhythm needed to pull the plough in a straight line, and would end up dragging each other around in circles. Instead of working together in unity, they were at odds with each other.

Many learn the hard way that our worldview matters a lot in business and that being *unequally yoked* can cause us to live with the frustration of being constantly at odds with our partner, or to cave in on our beliefs due to the pressure created by conflict. Unfortunately, it is most often the Christian who is pressured to compromise his or her faith, rather than the non-Christian, and this can set the business on a different course than was originally intended.

It's important to note that the verse above does not tell us to avoid non-Christians altogether! How can we be the salt and light of the world if we do? (1 Corinthians 5:9-10) However, we must realise that partnerships (especially legally binding ones) essentially strap individuals together and either add to or alleviate the burden being carried. Such a commitment is not easy to break, comes at high risk and should be entered into carefully and prayerfully.

When you are considering partnerships with someone who does not share the same beliefs, please take Paul's words seriously regarding the inherent risks. Once again, there is a simple solution to avoiding the worst-case scenario: evaluate potential partnerships through the lens of the Cause and ask yourself this question: Will this partnership help to bear the load of seeing the Cause fulfilled through the business, or will it pull it away from the God-given vision?

If the negative is true, let it go.

The Unreliable Lens

I hope you are beginning to see how viewing your life as a whole through the lenses of PURPOSE and CAUSE can bring about the kind of focus that yields great results and minimises the tug of war that you may be experiencing. However, there is another lens that is familiar to us all and can war against our ability to remain focussed. While at face value it can provide great benefits, when used as a lens it can distort our vision and distract us from our purpose.

I am referring to the lens of OPPORTUNITY.

Opportunity is a lens that many professionals choose to view life through. Hear me when I say that opportunity is an incredible thing and that I subscribe to the well-known saying, "The opportunity of a lifetime is found in the lifetime of the opportunity." However, the hard truth is that opportunity is an *unreliable* lens.

Take Jack for example—a workaholic businessperson who finally decides to follow through with a promise he made to take his young family on holiday. While on holiday, Jack is presented with a new, time-sensitive work opportunity that requires his immediate attention. Despite his wife's protests, Jack feels justified in abandoning 'family time' to attend to the opportunity because he sees every opportunity as a door to a more secure future. Sadly, many years later, Jack's family is no longer around him when that future finally becomes a reality.

In this example, the lens of opportunity distorted Jack's vision and took him away from God's best for his life.

I love a particular story of David and King Saul in the Bible, found in 1 Samuel 24. David had served King Saul faithfully for many years before the king became insecure and jealous of his accomplishments and turned on him. David was forced into hiding as King Saul pursued him with the intent to eliminate the great threat to the throne that he perceived David to be.

When the king entered a cave to relieve himself, David's men encouraged him to seize the opportunity and kill him while he was alone and vulnerable. Having been anointed to be king as a young boy, David knew that his purpose was to sit on Saul's throne in the timing of God. His men reminded him of that purpose and urged him to take the throne—by force—that very day.

Remarkably, despite the fact that he had been unjustly persecuted by a king that he loved and served, and was in fear for his life, David remained honourable and did not seize the opportunity that presented itself. He refused to reach out and prematurely take what God had covenanted to give him at the *right* time.

This remarkable story illustrates the mindset of a true king so well. David understood his purpose and confidently awaited the right moment to receive the throne that God had prepared for him. The opportunity to kill Saul could easily have stolen his focus and led him off-course from his destiny and purpose. As we see later in the story, the throne came to him as prophesied, and he was able to ascend it with clean hands and a pure heart.

Had David not had a clear sense of identity and purpose, he would have compromised his destiny by overlooking his integrity for a moment of opportunity. This is the behaviour of a dictator: take what you can when you can, regardless of the cost. While a king is driven by cause and purpose, a dictator is driven by insecurity and self-interest. One has a clear focus while the other blindly follows every opportunity that presents itself. If the situation were reversed, King Saul's identity crisis and insecurity would have driven him to take advantage of this 'too good to be true' opportunity to eliminate his rival and maintain a position of power.

While a king is driven by cause and purpose, a dictator is driven by insecurity and self-interest.

David's kingly mindset allowed him to focus on God's Cause and purpose when tempted to take the shortcut that this opportunity offered him.

What about promotion in the workplace? Time and time again I have seen good men and women view promotion through the lens of opportunity without giving it due thought and consideration. Sometimes they even uproot their families in pursuit of new business opportunities. So often, years after, I hear stories of how their children who once loved God and their local church, struggled to connect to a new church and ended up turning away from their faith. The one who pursued the promotion usually feels huge guilt and regret because they did not consider the full effects that the opportunity might have on their family. Whatever increase came, it was overshadowed by the huge and lasting cost to family and relationships.

Had they viewed the opportunity through the lenses of the Cause of Christ and of their divine purpose, they might have had the will and strength to make the hard, but RIGHT, decision of declining it.

There are many lenses like this that can distort our vision, undermine our cause and rob us of our unique purpose—not only for our business, but for every area of our lives.

My experience is that when you make the decision to view yourself as a king mandated for ministry in the marketplace, you begin to carry and present yourself differently and opportunity is magnetically attracted to you. I have seen this happen time and time again as individuals testify to the profound changes that happened as a result of positioning themselves for Kingdom-purpose. However, those who have been in the game long enough will tell you that not every opportunity is right for you. In fact, the very same opportunities that present themselves as a blessing can become your undoing if they are not part of God's purpose for your life.

The enemy loves to create chaos and confusion, and that chaos can sometimes look like God's blessing. When we embrace too many opportunities at the same time, or opportunities that steer us away from our core business and calling, we can end up being completely ineffective at doing anything at all. Our once *singular* focus becomes divided or distorted and we quickly lose sight of the thing we were called to do. Don't get me wrong, diversity is not bad in itself, but it is a double-edged sword—it can give us the power to take territory, and potentially wound us at the same time. It requires great wisdom to manage well.

If any of you lacks wisdom, you should ask God, who gives generously to all without finding fault, and it will be given to you. But when you ask, you must believe and not doubt, because the one who doubts is like a wave of the sea, blown and tossed by the wind. That person should not expect to receive anything from the Lord. Such a person is double-minded and unstable in all they do.

— James 1:5-8 (NIV)

Regardless of our natural ability or experience in the marketplace, we ALL need the wisdom of God to navigate life well. From the verse above, we can see that God is ready and willing to provide all of the wisdom we need—but there is a catch: we must BELIEVE and not DOUBT. Doubting God, His Word and His promises in our lives causes us to be 'double-minded' and 'unstable' in all of our ways, and this kind of instability is a deal-breaker for God.

God knows that when our vision has become blurred, we are unable to make sound, faith-based decisions that are God-honouring, or effectively steward the increase that He desires to deposit in our lives. By definition, doubt is a 'divided mind', and division always causes kingdoms to fall and not stand.

> *If a kingdom is divided against itself, that kingdom cannot stand.*
>
> *— Mark 3:24 (NIV)*

Essentially, the scripture is warning us that if we doubt God and His plans for our life, we shouldn't bother asking Him for anything at all! God's Kingdom is built through unity and agreement—starting with unity and agreement within our own self. When we are not in agreement with ourselves about our divine purpose, the result is living with blurred vision and with it—a tangible lack of peace, fulfilment and fruitfulness.

God's Word tells us that He is actively seeking people who are 'single-minded':

> *For the eyes of the Lord range throughout the earth to strengthen those whose hearts are fully committed to him.*
>
> *— 2 Chronicles 16:9 (NIV)*

In this context, the word 'committed' has the sense of being at rest because of a singular focus on, or devotion to God. In other words, God is actively seeking out people who have a clear and singular focus on Him so that He can strengthen them and bring increase to their lives.

Double-mindedness will prevent us from becoming all that God has called us to be. It will stand as a roadblock on the journey to our purpose and destiny, stealing joy, hope, faith and every other gift that God has promised for our lives. The same is true in the reverse. The man or woman who does not doubt God is SINGLE-MINDED (focussed) and should expect to receive ALL that they have asked for that fits into His will for their lives. Wow!

So the real question here is, how do we ensure that we are single-minded and focussed in our lives, positioning ourselves for the blessing and favour of God?

The answer? Believe and do not doubt.

Stay in Your Lane

Most professionals begin their journey single-minded. They are well acquainted with their strengths, gifts and talents and have a clear vision for their future. But somewhere along the journey, success creates opportunities and opportunities lure them away from their original vision and into areas where they have little or no experience. This distracts them from focussing on their core business and everything begins to unravel. Opportunities may seem lucrative or interesting, but like bait on the line, these businesspeople are snared and find themselves drawn away from their primary purpose.

In an interview with Craig Groeschel entitled 'Vision for the Future', author, teacher and leadership expert, Michael Hyatt, put it this way:

> **"When you become successful, opportunities show up at your doorstep. The problem is that distractions also show up masquerading as opportunity. The only way to tell the difference is when you have clarity around your vision. Your actions must align with your vision or you will get a lot of sideways energy that keeps people busy and overwhelmed, but does not drive towards the vision."**

Do you know what kind of business you are called to build or what role you are called to play in the marketplace? Are you single-minded in that focus?

We know from the Parable of the Talents that God values *stewardship* very much. He expects the gifts we have been given to be multiplied and rewards us with more when we work diligently to increase what we have. I have seen many businesspeople move from idea to idea, focus to focus, never fully investing in one area enough to see it grow and bring about a good return. This is not good stewardship!

Imagine if we had that attitude towards our spouses, children or jobs—moving from one to another and never putting in the effort to see the original 'gift' established to the point of flourishing! Imagine if we planted an apple tree and watched it grow for one month. However, seeing no fruit on it, we stop caring for it and move on to another tree. Sounds ridiculous right? Fruit is the END product of investing time, energy and resources into something you believe in. It takes time, focus, and faith to believe that it will bear fruit because that is its destiny. The same is true of kings in the marketplace.

I finish with a funny experience that taught me an important lesson about the power of focus.

I once decided to take my family out to watch a movie at the IMAX theatre in our city. The screen was absolutely huge—apparently the largest in the Southern Hemisphere—and we were really excited about watching the latest release called 'Aquaman'.

Just as the movie began, a fly flew onto the lens of the movie camera in the projector room which magnified it significantly as its image was projected onto the screen before our eyes. At first, the situation was quite entertaining, but when a second fly joined the first and could be seen flying around the screen, the distraction became too much. People began pointing and whispering, obviously agitated and distracted from the movie that had started. Eventually, several people stood up and left the room—presumably to alert staff to the problem—and a short time later, the flies disappeared. Unfortunately, the movie had been running for 10 minutes and I had allowed myself to become so distracted by the flies, that I missed the critical first moments of the story.

I share this as a warning to us all that distractions WILL come in many forms and have the power to blur our vision to the extent that we miss the main story that is playing out before us. It wasn't my fault that the flies entered my vision, but it WAS my choice to allow them to steal my focus and distort my ability to see the main story that was playing out before me.

We all have a choice as to what we will focus on and what lens we will view our story through.

We all have a choice to remain single-focussed or allow distractions to blur our vision and ability to interpret information accurately and make wise decisions that keep us on course to destiny.

SCAN & WATCH

What is the lens through which you are bringing focus to your life and business? Is it clarifying or distorting your focus?

PARTNERING WITH YOUR PASTOR

SCAN & WATCH

While the power of focus is crucial to fulfilling your purpose as a marketplace minister, it is all too easy to become tunnel-visioned in your pursuit of success and influence. I have seen too many businesspeople end up in places they never intended because their blindspots steered them off course over time. This is where transparency and submission to spiritual leadership is so important.

As we've talked about earlier in this book, EVERY Christian is called to be a minister of the Gospel in our various spheres of influence. But make no mistake, while ministry must go *beyond* the four walls of the Church, there is also a specific purpose for ministry *within* the four walls of the Church.

Paul puts it this way:

> **So Christ himself gave the apostles, the prophets, the evangelists, the pastors and teachers, to equip his people for works of service, so that the body of Christ may be built up until we all reach unity in the faith and in the knowledge of the Son of God and become mature, attaining to the whole measure of the fullness of Christ.**
> **— Ephesians 4:11-13 (NIV)**

We see here that those who are called to the office (duties) of a pastor, have a very clear heavenly mandate; to help God's people mature in their faith and to prepare them for service. Their purpose is to teach, preach, correct, disciple, lead, restore, rebuke, love and serve God's people—and that includes YOU.

This is a good moment to remind you that God's Church is not a democracy. Ultimately, the Church is led by God, who uses the spiritual leaders that He has appointed to partner with Him in guiding His people and advancing His Kingdom.

Hebrews 13:17 (NIV) commands us to, "Have confidence in your leaders and submit to their authority, because they keep watch over you as those who must give an account. Do this so that their work will be a joy, not a burden, for that would be of no benefit to you". While it is true that we now have DIRECT access to God ourselves, the principle of 'spiritual authority' is still relevant and crucial to our lives today.

Authority is a powerful principle that undergirds order on the Earth. Like it or not, each one of us must surrender to it daily on many various levels, in order to live and operate harmoniously alongside others. God Himself remains the ultimate authority in our lives. His authority is unmatched. Having given us the privilege of free will, He holds us accountable for our words, decisions and actions.

Human authority, on the other hand, is far more unstable and can be established in several different ways. It can be earned—as a result of expertise and excellence in a particular field. It can be taken—by force for the purpose of control (as in the case of a dictator). It can be entrusted—willingly gifted by those who are prepared to submit to it (as in the case of elected officials) and it can be delegated—as is the case when someone assigns their authority to another for a particular purpose.

There is one expression of authority that is crucial to your development as Christian marketplace leaders. I'm referring to the offices of authority that God appoints within His Church, the Body of Christ and His Kingdom, to lead and guide His people and to see His will outworked on the Earth.

True Submission

So what does it mean for a Christian professional to submit to spiritual authority? Well, to start with, I can tell you what it doesn't mean. It doesn't mean mindlessly obeying your pastor's every command or unconditionally accepting everything that you are told. Every believer is responsible to evaluate everything they hear in light of God's Word and to respond accordingly.

True submission is an attitude of the heart. It requires humility and recognising that we need God and others in our life. It is an awareness of and honour for those who God has positioned around us with the spiritual insight and wisdom that we will need in order to succeed in our pursuits and reach our full potential.

Submitting to spiritual authority is not always easy, especially for those who enjoy positions of authority and influence in their own right. Sometimes the problem is historical. Some have been hurt, misunderstood or taken for granted by pastors and church leaders in the past, and as a result, approach such relationships with caution. Despite the fact that most church leaders love their church and its people and genuinely want to do what is right, they are, nonetheless, human and fallible—as we all are. Disappointment and hurt is inevitable in relationships and this experience is certainly not unique to the church world.

Others submit to their pastor conditionally. While they are happy to follow them when they are in agreement with their decisions, they believe that their leader forfeits his or her authority when they do not agree, not realising that true submission of the heart can only be tested when we actually disagree.

Still others find it hard to submit to their pastor or leader due to his or her age, race, education, experience or personality— just to name a few factors. We only have to look to the Bible for many examples of God choosing the most outwardly unqualified individuals to occupy positions of great authority and influence. Clearly, He was more interested in the heart than the talent, and was well able to supernaturally equip His chosen ones for the service He had called them to.

More often than not, the root cause for a struggle to submit to spiritual authority is simple, but ugly and very destructive:

PRIDE.

Pride is a thief that keeps us from receiving what we need to succeed.

Pride is a thief that keeps us from receiving what we need to succeed. Our pride tells us that we do not need help and are wiser and more skilled than those who God has positioned to lead us. When we become proud and critical of our leaders, we are not walking in love and submission, but are instead positioning ourselves for a fall.

> *A man's pride and sense of self-importance*
> *will bring him down,*
> *But he who has a humble spirit will obtain honor.*
> — *Proverbs 29:23 (AMP)*

Alignment That Attracts

You might recall that in the chapter, 'Winning Cities', we talked about the power of *magnetism* that comes into play where there is *alignment*. This is just as relevant when it comes to unity between you and your church leaders. Let me remind you again that it is so important not to let differences of opinion cause disunity and rob you and your church of the blessing that God has for you. All too often it is pride that is the culprit when people refuse to set aside their differences.

Let's consider a common example. Perhaps you disagree with the way your church is managing its funds and it is causing you to become critical and disconnected from your pastor and church community. Maybe you are even right and could do a better job, but just because you are right does not mean that you have God's permission to dishonour those who are in authority. While God may give you the opportunity to share your insights and even bring help and support in this area, it is not primarily your job. Your responsibility is to be planted in the House of God (Psalm 92:13), submit to authority (Hebrews 13:17), not to neglect meeting together (Hebrews 10:25) and not to become weary in doing good (Galatians 6:9).

When you allow your disagreement to stop you from doing what you are called to do, then you come out of alignment with your purpose and with the spiritual family God has placed you in. But when you choose to get past your points of disagreement and focus on the big picture of the common cause, then, like the particles in a magnetized rod, there is an alignment that comes with a powerful force of attraction.

So here is the question: Even when you are in the right, will you hold onto your pride or will you choose to let it go for the sake of unity and the God-ordained blessing it attracts?

David or Saul?

David was a king who understood the power of submission to spiritual leadership. Despite his natural power and authority, he exhibited a rare humility when it came to seeking God's will for his life. Though fallible and prone to life-defining judgement errors, David understood that his kingship rose and fell with the will of God, and remained submitted to God and God's representatives on Earth (the prophets and the Levitical priesthood at the time) throughout his reign.

Even though he was a great king, a mighty warrior and master strategist, David understood that he was completely dependent on God for the longevity and success of His reign.

> *You, God, are my God, earnestly I seek you; I thirst for you, my whole being longs for you.*
>
> — *Psalm 63:1 (NIV)*

David modelled the posture of humility and submission to God and spiritual authority to his son Solomon, who himself went on to become a revered, successful and favoured king. Though both kings ruled imperfectly, God saw their hearts, honoured their intentions and blessed their respective reigns.

On the other hand, we see many biblical examples of kings who either rejected God or gradually became distant and apathetic towards Him— usually during seasons of success and peace. As they lost sight of the fact that their success was actually the result of God's intervention and protection, they often fell into independence and human reasoning— many times with devastating results for their kingdom and reign.

One of the clearest examples of this (and there are many) is David's predecessor, King Saul. Whereas David's reign was characterised by humility and obedience to God's instructions, Saul's reign was characterised by insecurity that was born out of pride. His downfall as king was the direct result of his failure to heed and obey God's instructions through the prophet-priest Samuel.

> *Because you have rejected the word of the Lord, He has also rejected you from being king.*
>
> — *1 Samuel 15:23 (NKJV)*

Saul's reply to these words is telling, as it unmasks the root of the problem:

> **Then Saul said to Samuel, "I have sinned. I violated the Lord's command and your instructions. I was afraid of the men and so I gave in to them.'"**
>
> — *1 Samuel 15:24 (NIV)*

The stress of Saul's position had become too much for him, causing his faith in God to waver. Saul's fear led him to ignore God's instruction and rely on his own understanding and analysis of the situation. The consequences of his refusal to heed God's Word through Samuel were devastating. Not only did he lose his position and influence, but he lost the battle (1 Samuel 31:3-6), and he along with his sons (the next generation) and many others, lost their lives.

Those who have ascended to positions of influence in the marketplace today understand that the higher and more responsible the leadership position, the greater the pressure. Most manage this pressure in one of two ways: they either look for ways to control their circumstances as best they humanly can, or they relinquish control and look to God for the strength, wisdom and the resources they need to fulfil their purpose with grace and integrity. The latter requires humility and faith—two things that can be the most challenged in our journey of kingship.

Just like our predecessor King David, great 'kings' still willingly submit to spiritual guidance today out of security in their identity and calling. They feel safe when opening up their lives and revealing vulnerability to their spiritual leaders because their position is secure and does not need to be protected. They remain focussed on their kingly purpose and understand the role of God-ordained partnerships in their quest for success. They do not see their need for others as a sign of weakness, but as an integral strategy for success.

Dictators, on the other hand, because of pride and insecurity, are typically all about control and see submission as vulnerability. Ironically, because of fear, they elevate themselves to the position of a god, bowing down at the altar of their own ego and ambition. We can all fall into this way of thinking when we are immersed in an 'every man for himself' culture daily. Our simple faith and trust in God can falter when we see others appear to thrive and prosper in environments of control, manipulation and corruption. What we don't often get to see is the fruit that inevitably forms in these lives down the track, when the empty wisdom of godless culture proves to be unreliable and at times, corrupting.

The question is: What kind of leader are you? Do you habitually look to God for guidance or revert to your own wisdom and instincts?

The Matter of Control

Many successful Christian professionals are fully committed to their churches, giving generously of their time and resources but never reaching the point of totally surrendering their businesses to God. Only a few live with the revelation that the call of God to the ministry of business will cost them something that is very precious—CONTROL. Those who yield to the call and lay their businesses on the altar before God, recognise that in doing so, they are no longer the boss and look to God for His will in every decision.

Those who yield to the call and lay their businesses on the altar before God, recognise that in doing so, they are no longer the boss and look to God for His will in every decision.

One of the most important decisions you'll ever make is whether or not you choose to partner with your local church and pastor, or live your life independent from the vehicle God has chosen to build His Kingdom on Earth.

Having personally operated in both the business and church arenas of life, I believe with all of my heart that partnerships between the two are powerful, essential and mutually beneficial to those who are called by God to operate in each. Without such partnerships, the Church cannot grow at the pace God desires it to and businesses cannot thrive and flourish to the level He intended. Just as He Himself chose to partner with mankind to rule over Creation, God continues to seek out partnerships that He can bless, empower, equip and deploy to advance His Kingdom.

As marketplace leaders, if we are going to embrace partnership with our pastors, it is really important that we understand their role in our lives.

We have already discussed the fact that the role of our pastors is no longer to stand BETWEEN us and God—in a mediatory role—but instead, to walk ALONGSIDE us on our journey, encouraging and guiding us so that we stay on course in our faith and fulfil our God-given destiny. Their job is to seek the heart of God and to empower and equip us with God's Word so that we can flourish and prosper in every area of our lives, and grow in spiritual maturity.

Biblically, the word 'pastor' simply means 'shepherd'. Our pastors are called to care for and guide us through life, feeding us spiritually and protecting us from any danger they see ahead for our lives. They are also called to be 'nurturers', supporting us through all of life's circumstances and being ready and able to instruct us concerning the powerful application of God's Word in our lives. There is absolutely NO doubt that we need them—even when we feel invincible, successful and in control. In fact, these are the times we need them the most!

Welcome to the Game

I like to use the analogy of a sports coach and their team when discussing the potential relationship between professionals and their pastors.

Every team needs a coach. Without a coach, unity and teamwork are impossible to achieve. In any team context, leadership is crucial to the success and fruitfulness of that team; and in the church context, our pastors occupy that leadership role.

The Bible is clear that ALL authority that exists in our lives, has been appointed by God.

The Bible is clear that ALL authority that exists in our lives, has been appointed by God—a truth that is often very difficult to swallow:

> *Let everyone be subject to the governing authorities, for there is no authority except that which God has established. The authorities that exist have been established by God.*
>
> *— Romans 13:1 (NIV)*

Sometimes we may question the credentials of our pastors and their competency to lead us, and find it difficult to submit to their leadership when we believe they lack knowledge, wisdom or experience in an area. Though this is a common problem for everyone, submitting to those in authority over us is not negotiable in the eyes of God and is one of the greatest tests of our faith in His leadership. It is so important that we see our pastors and the authority they carry through God's eyes and not through the eyes of the corporate world.

During a big sporting game, coaches often employ a 'set play' tactic. A set play is a set of movements that can be planned on paper and practised, allowing the team to position themselves in the best possible way to score. Set plays are rehearsed many times over during training to make sure that every player knows exactly what to do, where they should be positioned and what is expected of them in order to maximise the potential to score and win. Without these set plays, in the high-pressure moments of the game when players are feeling stressed and fatigued, poor decisions can be made that negatively affect the outcome for everyone.

I strongly believe that our pastors fill the role of coach in our lives and are equipped and anointed by God to position and prepare us to use our gifts and talents to maximum potential. Winning is dependent then on each one of us understanding our position and purpose on the team, and our ability to hear and obey the voice of our coach/pastor when the game is on!

So often, professionals know exactly what to do in the context of their businesses, which is why they are so successful. They instinctively know when to act and when to wait; when to speak up and when to shut up; when to offer advice and when to bow out; when to spend and when to invest. These are the set plays that become so familiar with experience and play out time and time again. They are learned by making mistakes in the beginning—many times serious, life-defining mistakes—but pressing on to learn from those mistakes and to respond differently during the next 'game'.

However, when it comes to their spiritual lives and their relationship with their local church and pastor, the 'set play' is often not as clear and instinctive for professionals. What do you do when you see your church floundering financially or struggling to make a business-related decision that you feel you have the answer to? Can you speak up? Should you speak up? Do you just give the money to resolve a problem or offer advice that might stop the problem from ever happening again? What is the RIGHT thing to do?

The feelings of powerlessness and uncertainty that are often felt by professionals in the arena of church life often causes them to withdraw from the game altogether—never experiencing the satisfaction of winning that belongs to players and not spectators. That is why it is so important that we actively seek to build relationship with our pastor/coach, and learn to trust in their spiritual leadership—allowing ourselves to be positioned and trained to respond to the set plays that are needed for Kingdom expansion.

However, even the most talented team training under the most experienced coach is destined to fail unless each of its members are equally committed to unity and agreement!

An Attractive Sound

Matthew 18:19 presents us with an incredible promise regarding unity:

> *Again I say to you, that if two believers on earth agree [that is, are of one mind, in harmony] about anything that they ask [within the will of God], it will be done for them by My Father in heaven.*
>
> *— Matthew 18:19 (AMP)*

Clearly, God is offering free and unlimited access to the treasures of Heaven, with only two conditions attached:

1. That what we ask for falls within His will
2. That at least two believers AGREE about what they are asking for

It sounds so simple, yet we all know that both of these conditions require effort on our part.

Firstly, in order to really know and understand God's will, we must know HIM intimately, and this is only achieved as we dedicate time to spend with Him in prayer, in worship and in His Word. Time is one of the most precious and limited resources in the life of most professionals. To invest it in seeking God is something we must decide to do as a priority, long before the normal pressures and stresses of corporate life fight for our time and attention.

Secondly, and even more challenging, is that we must learn what it means to really agree with another believer—a faith action that goes deeper than superficially agreeing with a person in order to please them and avoid conflict.

The word 'agree' in the above verse comes from the original Greek term, 'symphonia', meaning—to 'harmonise'. It is where we get the term 'symphony' from which is a musical composition written for a full orchestra. The quality of any orchestra is completely dependent on the ability of each musician to play their individual part competently, in time with the other musicians in the orchestra and in perfect pitch so as to blend in seamlessly and not produce a sound that clashes with other instruments and ruins the entire performance. No one attends a concert for this kind of experience—unless you are a dedicated parent of a child who plays in an amateur band!

Although there are moments when an individual musician may perform a short solo that draws attention to themselves and their skills, an orchestra is generally celebrated for the combined talents of all of its musicians who work hard to flow together in perfect harmony at all times. In the context of an orchestra, the conductor is the 'coach' and success depends on every individual musician following their leader.

> *Does not the potter have the right to make out of the same lump of clay some pottery for special purposes and some for common use?*
>
> *— Romans 9:21 (NIV)*

The importance of this analogy is the willingness of each individual player to lay down their right to personal glory in order to agree and harmonise with other musicians for the common purpose of producing a beautiful corporate sound.

This kind of harmony is what God desires to 'hear' in the relationships between professionals and their pastors. In fact, the sound that is emitted when His people are in unity together over things that fall within His will is so attractive and irresistible to God that He has promised to respond with 'commanded blessing' every time He hears it!

> *How good and pleasant it is*
> *when God's people live together in unity!*
> *It is like precious oil poured on the head,*
> *running down on the beard,*
> *running down on Aaron's beard,*
> *down on the collar of his robe.*
> *It is as if the dew of Hermon*
> *were falling on Mount Zion.*
> *For there the Lord bestows his blessing,*
> *even life forevermore.*
>
> — *Psalm 133 (NIV)*

When both the pastor and businessperson choose to agree on things that fall within the boundaries of His will, God promises that absolutely NOTHING will be impossible or withheld from His hand. This is a powerful promise that allows His Kingdom to expand without resistance when we choose unity above our own rights and opinions.

On the other hand, where there is no agreement, pastors and businesspeople are so often left shipwrecked in a raging sea of differing opinions and perspectives.

Dead in the Water

Over many years working alongside people of all walks of life, it never ceases to frustrate me when I see so much God-given vision never actually come to pass. There is no shortage of vision as God is constantly talking to us all, stirring our faith to believe for more. So why does so much vision fall to the ground over time?

Perhaps the problem is that we sometimes fail to find the true agreement needed in order to release the commanded blessing and activate the vision in our lives, our families, our businesses and our churches.

The truth is that choosing to agree will often mean laying aside our personal opinion and to instead agree by faith with another's vision in order to activate the commanded blessing of God. This is never easy and does not always make sense, but it is deeply important to God. He is more interested in the condition of our hearts than the content of our minds, and our relationships with Him and each other reflect of the true condition of our hearts at any given time.

You may have heard the saying used frequently in the business world, "*Partnerships are sinking ships.*" Clearly this was coined by someone who experienced disappointment in the area of business partnerships. The truth is that we have all experienced failure in partnerships of different kinds. Partnering with others—whether in business, marriage or church life—is challenging and demands that we yield a level of control and embrace difference. Very often, these partnerships start off strong and full of potential, but get bogged down in the mud and are unable to advance when opposing views are presented and no one is willing to compromise or yield for the purpose of agreement. The consequences of reaching a stalemate situation like this can be devastating, particularly when much resource (time, money, emotion etc.) has been invested.

Negative experiences with partnerships that didn't work out can make us reluctant to try again. But when we dig a little deeper, this reluctance is just *fear*—the greatest enemy of our faith. Rather than following our gut instinct to retreat, build walls and 'go it alone', a faith-filled approach would be to learn something about ourselves and what went wrong so that future partnerships can be successful and fruitful. Whether we like it or not, partnerships are a non-negotiable Kingdom strategy for success!

> *Two are better than one, because they have a good return for their labor...*
>
> *— Ecclesiastes 4:9 (NIV)*

Counting the Cost

The decision to partner with your pastor can so easily be made with the right intention, but also with inadequate consideration of what such a partnership will cost you personally. Truly agreeing with your pastor involves a decision of the heart that when all is said and done, and when all arguments have been presented, you still choose to agree regardless of whether or not your desires have been met in the process. This kind of agreement is deep, powerful and pleasing to God. It doesn't mean that you will always have the same opinions, but it does mean that you are prepared to yield in order to settle on an outcome by focussing on the vision and the relationship, moving forward and enjoying the benefits of God's commanded blessing!

Walking together in relationship implies that our lives are entwined and interdependent with a mutual commitment to the health of that relationship. Effort is required to maintain, and at times repair, the relationship when the journey unexpectedly encounters resistance. Sadly, many people conduct their relationships like two trains running on parallel train tracks that never have to meet, touch or adjust their course to accommodate the other. Many marriages I have encountered are like this. As long as they are travelling in the same direction and towards the same destination, they believe their relationship is strong and functional.

Many pastors and businesspeople find this kind of relationship the easiest to achieve and maintain because there is less likelihood of conflict and tension. Both sides maintain control of their engine at all times while enjoy the company of the other from a safe distance. Sadly, they miss out on the power that comes with true partnerships which demand a higher level of vulnerability, authenticity, discipleship, accountability and dying to self for the sake of the other. As with any business endeavour in life, hard work, risk and commitment are required in order to achieve success—but few are willing to pay the price. It is our natural tendency to want the benefits of lasting relationship, without making the commitment required to build it brick by brick!

The only way we will truly see the incredible plans of God fulfilled in our lifetime is when we ALL make a genuine, well-considered commitment of our hearts to stand in agreement—pastors and professionals together— and take our place in the 'orchestra' that God has planted us in.

Let's look a little deeper at the operation of an orchestra to really unravel the meaning of 'agreement' as it applies to the relationship between marketplace leaders and their pastors.

Accepting Your Part

In any orchestra, each individual musician is appointed to play a certain part. They are each selected according to their instrument and skill level, and each part is vitally important to the overall sound.

Not only must each musician understand their individual part, but also how their part fits into the overall musical score. When they are fully familiar with the part they have been appointed to play, all that is left to do is to practice in private until they have perfected it before joining the entire orchestra to rehearse the piece together as a whole.

As a Christian professional, do you understand the part you are called to play (and hence the position you are called to occupy) in producing a 'symphony' of harmonised sound in the Kingdom and in your church?

For some of you, the idea of becoming more involved in the vision of your church is a brand new concept, while for others, it can be quite an overwhelming one given the pace at which you already live life in the business world. But maybe you've already reached your potential as a soloist and are ready to become part of something bigger—a greater sound that has even greater influence.

Most of you clearly understand the role you play in your business, but have no idea how this role could be utilised in the church setting. This is where your partnership with your pastor comes into play. Like the conductor of the orchestra or the coach of the team, your pastor will work with you to discover the unique part God is calling you to play.

Like the coach of the team, your pastor will work with you to discover the unique part God is calling you to play.

Performance-Ready

Before an orchestra can ever learn to harmonise together, each individual musician must pursue excellence by practising their instrument in private. In fact, the conductor relies on this. When the orchestra comes together, there is no time for individual practice. Unless individual practice has been done in private by the musicians, the orchestra will never achieve its collective potential. In the same way, if you, as a professional, fail to give sufficient time, attention and focus to developing your business skills, you will never be able to make the contribution to the Kingdom that God has called you to make. Yet, just as with the orchestra, true success is not about how great you can become as a soloist. Rather, it is about how you are positioned to contribute to the far greater collective vision that God has for His Kingdom on Earth.

Many years ago, I was invited by a business friend of mine to attend a Valentine's Day concert performed by the West Australian Symphony Orchestra, outdoors on the greens of his beautiful golf course. I admit, I was not a fan of orchestra music—but having a wife who was a musician, and given the perfect weather conditions and picturesque surroundings, I felt I might be on a romantic 'winner' and agreed to attend. I confess that I was dreading the 2-hour concert and hoped that the time would pass quickly.

It was a beautiful balmy night and my friend had generously allowed us to sit amongst the VIPs, enjoying gourmet snacks and sitting on comfortable chairs as the orchestra began to play. To my shock, the amazing, harmonious sound of the orchestra really moved me. Before the night was over, I was making plans to attend the following year!

I wonder if my experience would have been different if some of the musicians had failed to practice and made noticeable mistakes as the orchestra played? What if some had assumed that they didn't need to practise because their job was secure and they were confident that they could bluff their way through it? What if some were jealous of others and deliberately played louder and more forcefully than they should, just to be noticed by the crowd? What if some left early before the performance was over because they lost interest or felt unappreciated? Worst of all, what if some of these musicians couldn't stand their conductor and refused to follow his direction, playing what they thought was better in the moment?

The truth is, despite disliking this kind of music, I was drawn in and convinced to return for future performances because I experienced an orchestra that was perfectly harmonised and unified. The same is true of the partnerships that we make in our lives—especially with our pastors and church teams. They WILL make a sound, but the question is whether or not that sound will be attractive to the listener!

So I ask you now, what sound are you emitting in your home, your church and your business? Do you know your part? Are you in your right position? Have you practiced enough? Have you chosen to come into agreement and harmony with those on your team? Have you surrendered yourself to the leadership of your conductor and coach? Are you ready to bring the performance of your life in the moment of your opportunity?

Hopefully I have inspired you to take your place in the 'orchestra' of Kingdom life and on the 'team' that God has prepared for you in a new, deeper and more committed way than ever before. Regardless of your previous experiences, I pray that your heart is open to the possibility of building a partnership with your pastor for the Cause of the Kingdom. Above all, I hope you have begun to see that you are called to be much more than just another professional focussed on building personal wealth.

That said, I may have also stirred up your concerns about adding a further commitment to your already hectic life!

Breaking the Camel's Back

Though most of us are energised by the idea of operating in our God-given calling, the reality of limited time, energy and focus plagues us all. How do we reconcile our call to marketplace ministry when we already work 80 hours a week and barely meet our family commitments? How do we move beyond feeling guilty and inadequate when commitment is talked about at church and we can't even commit to attending a small group? How do we show up to midweek night meetings at 7.30pm with a great attitude, when we have come straight from an exhausting and stressful day at the office?

With this kind of mental and physical stress in life, it is no wonder that professionals are often the loneliest people. It comes as no surprise that many choose to take a passive, back-seat approach to church life to avoid feeling like a failure by not meeting even more expectations! Others, in an attempt to meet their church commitments, drive themselves to work harder and give more—often to the detriment of their health, marriages and relationship with God.

This is a very real issue that needs to be resolved if we want to fully embrace our calling and destiny.

Getting your world in order begins by remembering that ministry in the marketplace is a CALLING and with every calling, we have a specific part to play. When we do not understand our specific role, we can so easily get caught up (whether self-imposed or pressured by others) trying to play the parts that have been set aside for others to play. Inevitably, we play them poorly. Therefore, we need to have a clear understanding of our role and clear boundaries within that role to protect us from living drained and unfulfilled spiritual lives.

The very same principles apply to pastors. They must understand their role and stay within the boundaries of that role so they can play their part to the best of their ability. Pastors are not called to give business advice to those they lead, nor are businesspeople to dictate the vision of the church. It is important to remember that our pastors are not our enemies, sent to load us up with more work, but are a gift from God to fulfil a vital role in our lives—helping us to succeed in every area. Likewise, businesspeople are a gift to their pastors, appointed by God to provide advice and supply resources to see the vision fulfilled.

Clearly defined roles are critical to the health and fruitfulness of your partnership with your pastor. Honour, respect, honesty, vulnerability, authenticity and grace should be the hallmarks of your partnership. If guilt, shame, manipulation, fear or dishonesty are in operation, then it's time to re-evaluate the roles that both you and your pastor have been playing.

Extending Grace

One of the revelations God gave me in my time as a senior pastor in observing the unique stresses faced by businesspeople and professionals, is that it's okay for them to live outside of the commitments that we tend to require of our faithful core. I know this is a controversial conversation, but one I believe needs to be had if we want businesspeople to take their God-ordained place on the team.

Long work hours and frequent travel commitments can make attending church events very challenging for professionals and interrupt the momentum that pastors are trying to build in the lives of the people they lead. In my experience, most businesspeople want to be a committed member of their church community and don't want to disappoint their pastors in any way, but there are challenges unique to their occupation that make it very difficult to be consistent.

On the other hand, I have also known many businesspeople who attend church only as an obligation to their family, have a very superficial relationship with God and genuinely look for opportunities NOT to take up their responsibilities in their spiritual family. These are not the kind of people I am talking about right now. Such people require discipleship to deepen their faith and pastors will need the wisdom of the Holy Spirit to keep them engaged and growing in their relationship with God. I am instead referring to those with a heart after God and a love for His House, but who simply struggle to make it all work together.

Likewise, most pastors don't want to place unnecessary stress on their people, but genuinely desire to build them up spiritually and activate them for Kingdom purpose. It is clear that most professionals and pastors don't mean to cause harm to each other, but instead need to learn how to understand each other and work together for mutual benefit.

During a sporting match, a gifted player may sit on the bench during most of the game, waiting for the moment when the coach calls them up. Having decided to enact a 'set play', the coach will call on the player who is most likely to orchestrate victory—due to their specific skill set—but this play may only take a few minutes of the entire game. In the same way, I believe that businesspeople may legitimately be excused from some general church activities that apply pressure to their lives beyond that experienced by others, so long as they are ready and willing to be called up to the plate at the moment their pastor and coach instigates a set play.

There is no desire in me to exempt businesspeople from the normal responsibilities of belonging to a church family, or from those activities that will help them grow spiritually and give sacrificially, but I do believe that wisdom and grace can and should be applied to their unique lives. When grace is extended in this way, it is my experience that they respond by bringing their best into the partnership they share with their pastors.

Who's Got You?

The truth is that professionals are often focussed on caring for the needs of their employees, shareholders, clients etc., but who is taking care of them?

Who truly cares about YOU—not your business, not your wealth, not what you can do for them or give to them...just YOU?

Who notices when you are feeling unusually stressed, discouraged, disappointed or worried about a big decision that needs to be made?

Who perceives that you and your wife are not travelling well and need help to navigate your relationship?

Who challenges you to slow down, take a holiday and look after your health?

Who offers themselves as a 'safe place' to express your feelings, emotions, hopes and dreams without judgement?

If the answer is "no one", maybe it's time to connect with your pastor and start building relationship.

The Underbelly of Success

Unfortunately, we live in a world that is preoccupied with self. Most successful professionals would understand that the *underbelly* of that success is being seen as a 'means to an end' for others. Even in church life, many businesspeople are forced to sift through potential friendships to find which is genuine and which is strategic for someone who is wanting to get to know them for personal gain. This can be painful and frustrating, but is to be expected in a fallen world. The real test is whether or not you can navigate church life without taking on offence and becoming a cynical person who struggles to build ANY meaningful relationships at all.

Many years ago when I was a senior pastor in Perth, Western Australia, I was recruited by some older pastors that I held in high esteem to head up our church movement. They approached me with enthusiasm, presenting me with the vision to re-energise an aging movement by bringing in a fresh, young man of God to orchestrate the change necessary for growth. I felt extremely honoured and took the position willingly. I gave that job my all, making changes I felt instructed by God to make and championing the cause of young, upcoming ministers.

Not long into my term, I was suddenly asked to step down from my position of authority, leaving me shocked and disappointed. It turned out that those older ministers who I trusted, wanted to maintain control while putting a young face to the leadership. I was to be a puppet. When I instigated radical change under the guidance of the Holy Spirit, they panicked, regretted their decision and discharged me of my duties.

At the time, this was a really painful and humiliating experience, but God used it to teach me some lessons I needed in preparation for the seasons ahead. The truth is that we live in a fickle world. Wisely navigating it and keeping our hearts pure is usually more productive than complaining about it and trying to change it. People will always do what they can to orchestrate their own plans—even if it involves using us for selfish gain—but their behaviour will never affect the plans God has for our lives when we choose to stay focussed on Him. However, when we take on offence and choose to stop trusting people because of a selfish few, we can delay what God wants to do in and through our lives because our hearts become hardened and our ears deaf to His leading.

This is where we need our coach/conductor to step into our lives, perceive where we're at and challenge us to keep our hearts soft and responsive to God. This kind of perceptiveness only comes as we develop relationship with our pastor over time, remaining vulnerable, honest and accountable. I thank God that He always provided a godly pastor to stand alongside me, even in my darkest times.

Impossible Possibilities

I hope it's clear now how important it is for you to build a partnership with your church and pastor. As the story of the Tower of Babel (Genesis 11:1-9) shows, when people came together in full agreement with one mind and one vision, they became unstoppable. On that occasion, the united effort of those building the tower caught God's attention. Having come down to see it for Himself, He declared that with such unity, nothing would be impossible for them to achieve. This principle is just as true for us today!

This is the invitation that is extended to all marketplace ministers. Will you stay focussed on building your own empire and acquiring personal wealth, or will you position yourselves in a God-centred team that shares the singular vision of seeing His Kingdom expanded? Will you view your business as the fruit of your own abilities and efforts, or as a tool God has gifted you for use in His Kingdom? Will you be content to witness the most incredible moves of God on Earth in your lifetime from a distance, or do you want to play in the game itself?

The truth is, you are critical to the extension of God's Kingdom on Earth—just as you are, in your role as a marketplace leader and member of the family of God. You do not need to work on a church staff or attend Bible College to please God or have lasting impact on the Earth for His Kingdom! In a typical church congregation, only 2% at most, will work on staff in a ministry capacity. We need YOU—the other 98%—to stand up and play your role in seeing the vision of your church fulfilled.

But make no mistake! You cannot do this alone.

I leave you with this simple question: Who is your spiritual coach?

BUILDING
A WINNING
TEAM

In previous chapters, I alluded to the fact that great kings do not rule in isolation. Rather, they surround themselves with trusted advisors FROM whom they can extract great wisdom and expertise, and TO whom they can delegate day-to-day responsibilities. In this way, a wise king is able to remain focussed on his personal mandate by allowing his vision to be sharpened by the wisdom of others and unburdened by things that others can oversee on his behalf.

A true king has enough humility to recognise that he is fallible and in need of many advisors.

A true king has enough humility to recognise that he is fallible and in need of many advisors in order to rule with integrity, wisdom and ultimately, success.

> *For lack of guidance a nation falls, but victory is won through many advisers.*
>
> *— Proverbs 11:14 (NIV)*

Secure in his inherited position, a good king is able to trust freely and relinquish control to others without fear of betrayal or loss. Dictators, on the other hand, surround themselves with 'yes men', who help them feel like they are in control. The team environment is generally one of mistrust, with differing opinions seen as disloyalty and a threat. Teams that surround dictators generally operate out of fear, jostling for positions of power and influence with a leader who generally only rewards those who agree with him. Only the strongest survive! This is NOT a healthy team as team members are never trusted to do what is right by the leader and the kingdom.

It goes without saying that if you intend to become an effective and successful marketplace minister, who you choose to surround yourself with will be a crucial indicator of how the endgame will look. Likewise, the team players you position alongside you will invariably determine just how enjoyable and rewarding the journey will be!

I have heard it said that it is teamwork that enables *ordinary* people to do *extraordinary* things.

Management consultant, educator and author, Peter Drucker, put it this way:

> **"No organisation can depend on genius; the supply is always scarce and unreliable. It is the test of an organisation to make ordinary human beings perform better than they seem capable of, to bring out whatever strength there is in its members, and to use each one's strength to help all the others perform. The purpose of an organisation is to enable *common people to do uncommon things*." (emphasis added)**

This quote resonates with me. When I think about where I would be without the teams of individuals who have surrounded my life like scaffolding on a building—filling the many gaps in my skills, reinforcing the weak areas and sharpening my cutting edge—I am humbled. Though I have received personal accolades for my achievements over the years, I am acutely aware that the real me is far less capable than the person I am perceived to be—thanks to the 'super' that my team adds to this 'man' on a daily basis!

One of the greatest challenges I see facing marketplace organisations today is the failure of their staff to function well as a team. So often, a few very gifted people carry the 'lion's share' of the load which results in inefficiency, burn out and in time, failure. No matter how gifted and capable individuals are, no one can truly perform to their maximum potential and achieve lasting success without the support of a great team around them.

Even a champion athlete who is at the top of their game in an individual sport such as sprinting or tennis, cannot truly achieve excellence without the constant support of an unseen team—each bringing their individual gifts and skills to the table to assist the athlete in achieving far more than they could on their own. Raw skill or 'genius' is not enough to ensure long-term success. In the life of an athlete, failure is only one serious injury away, so having a team of trainers around them to prevent such injuries and keep them functioning at their maximum potential is essential.

As always, Jesus set the example of embracing a team in every context of life. Being God Himself and carrying absolute power and authority, He could easily have completed His Father's agenda on Earth without any help whatsoever. He instead chose for Himself a team to assist Him to carry out His mandate. To the observer, the team He chose seemed less than ideal, but He saw potential in each one to contribute to the vision of establishing His Kingdom on Earth—even Judas. Jesus set about building relationship with His fledgling team, training them and delegating responsibilities until they became successful at turning the known world upside down with His message and establishing the New Testament Church.

Great Teamwork Begins with a Great Leader

In the previous chapter, we explored the critical importance of leadership in the team. The coach (or conductor) plays a crucial role in the performance of the team by bringing out the best in each team member and managing the team as a whole. Being the leader is a great privilege, but as any leader will tell you, it comes with great responsibility.

> *From everyone who has been given much, much will be demanded; and from the one who has been entrusted with much, much more will be asked.*
> — *Luke 12:48 (NIV)*

The key to great leadership is the awareness that growth, learning and change are life-long goals. The idea that we simply arrive at being a great leader only limits our potential in the long-term. Being a life-long learner takes great humility and commitment, and only the most mature leaders will continue this pursuit well after they have achieved a significant level of success.

> *A wise man will hear and increase learning, and a man of understanding will attain wise counsel.*
> — *Proverbs 1:5 (NKJV)*

Who are You Pursuing?

Great leaders are not intimidated by mixing with even greater leaders.

As we reflect on the most powerful and influential leaders on the world stage today, we can see that this kind of greatness is in short supply. The leadership of many is marked by insecurity that inevitably leads to conflict, fear-mongering and manipulation. Those who live and work under such leaders inevitably suffer the same fate and end up living with insecurity and fear themselves.

Great leaders are not intimidated by mixing with even greater leaders.

It is human nature to naturally mix with people who we feel in some way superior to. Hanging around less competent or experienced people than ourselves makes us feel secure, needed and accomplished. There is no competition or feelings of inadequacy in these environments. On the other hand, spending time with MORE competent and experienced people can have the opposite effect! We become aware of our inadequacies, tempted to compare ourselves with others and worried that our weaknesses may be exposed for all to see.

The truth is, if you genuinely want to be a great leader, you MUST spend time with leaders who have what you need. This means honestly evaluating where your weaknesses lie and what skills you need to develop.

You may be a gifted marketplace leader, but lack the accounting, administration, self-discipline or relational skills required to be truly successful. In my experience, many professionals in these situations work hard to hide their inadequacies—giving the appearance of being in control but seriously struggling behind the scenes. They tend to lack confidence, condemning themselves harshly for their failings, constantly comparing their performance with others and avoiding people who are naturally gifted in the area where they are weak—all the while allowing their business to struggle on, bearing the undealt-with brunt of their weaknesses. To be honest, this is simply PRIDE—the ultimate enemy of success. Pride stops you from acknowledging need: if you fail to deal with it, it will lead you away from your God-given purpose.

> *When pride comes, then comes disgrace, but with humility comes wisdom.*
> — *Proverbs 11:2 (NIV)*

Those leaders who achieve long-term success, find others who are strong in areas of their weakness and hang around them to glean from their skills and experience. They refuse to wallow in self-pity or allow their vulnerabilities to sabotage their success. They are quick to identify their weaknesses, secure in declaring them and humble enough to take lessons from others who are able to bring out the gold in them and unlock new opportunities. A lot of humility is required to surround yourself with bigger people—especially when you see yourself

A lot of humility is required to surround yourself with bigger people

as a king—but we shouldn't confuse this with weakness. Humility and strength go hand in hand—just look to King Jesus as the example of this in action!

I want you to consider for a moment how you feel when someone approaches you for help. We all love to be needed and are generally very happy to pour out our knowledge and experience on those who humbly seek it. Humility is a powerful key to unlock the treasure in another person's life, and our first response is rarely to judge them for declaring their weaknesses and asking for help. This is called 'discipleship'. When we give of ourselves in this way, we reflect the nature and glory of God in a way that is deeply satisfying. If we love helping people who approach us and draw wisdom out of us, how much more will others treat us in the same way when we ask them for help? Worrying about a person's opinion or judgement is a certain way to shut down your growth as a leader.

I have needed this kind of help from others constantly throughout my 30 years in the ministry. As a young pastor and leader, I was aware that my faith level was limiting the growth of my church, so I began looking for people who were more advanced in their faith and found ways to spend time with them. It was in those early days that I began building a friendship with Pastor Russell Evans who has always had a powerful ability to hear the voice of God and step out in faith. The more time I spent with him, the more inspired I became. I watched him in action and got to know him behind the scenes, and my faith began to grow. There is no doubt that the ridiculous level of faith that I now need to practise in my job daily, 30 years later, was developed in those early days when I dedicated myself to learning from someone who was more advanced in that area.

So I ask you: What are your weaknesses in business and life? Who are you pursuing in order to grow in those areas?

Let the Pendulum Swing

Many times we hide behind our personality as an excuse to not grow in certain areas—both personally and in business. As a young man, I was not particularly 'touchy-feely' and was unable to communicate the level of relational warmth needed to convey authentic love to the people of my church. I considered myself a 'man's man' and would cringe when grown men embraced each other affectionately and without restraint. Responding to the prompting of the Holy Spirit in my heart, I decided I needed to grow in this area—despite my genuine reservations!

I remember joining my staff for morning tea after a staff meeting one day and approaching two men who were sitting on either end of a three-seater couch. The only available seat was positioned intimately between the two. Contrary to my natural instinct, I planted myself in the middle and began to interact. I had to take what felt like an extreme measure in that moment to challenge my comfort level head-on so that I could begin to deconstruct old patterns of interactions and build new ones into my life.

I get that this is a strange illustration for some people—especially those who find affection easy and natural—but my point is that I had to allow the pendulum to swing a long way from my normal for a while, before it could settle somewhere in the middle. Many years later, after repeatedly and deliberately placing myself in uncomfortable situations, I can now report that I am extremely comfortable in expressing affection to men and women alike. This is my 'new normal', but it began by allowing the pendulum to swing to the far side of my natural personality.

The truth is, if you want to be a great leader and king in the marketplace, you will need to be willing to ignore your natural instincts, personality and comfort zones to develop the skills and attitudes that are currently lacking in your life and holding you back from operating at your full potential. Every natural king who has ever risen to a throne has done so bringing both the strengths and weaknesses of his DNA and upbringing with him. These factors must be confronted, accepted and eventually conquered by us all in our quest to rise to our ultimate calling. Weakness cannot be tolerated as a valid excuse for failure, but embraced as the territory in which God can be most glorified in our lives.

Consider for a moment King David who was just a boy when he took down Goliath; Moses who was called to deliver God's people, but could not speak clearly; Gideon who saw himself as the 'least of the least', yet stepped up to accept his God-given purpose; and Esther who was simply a beautiful young girl with the weight of her nation riding on her shoulders. Each testifies to the fact that God is attracted to weakness when it is surrendered to Him by faith.

Maybe you have a brilliant business mind that attracts big money, but lack the organisational or administrative skills needed to steward the wealth well. In my experience, many businesses that began full of potential end up floundering, not because they were not good at their core business, but because they allowed the wealth that was brought in to slip away due to mismanagement. Maybe if the leader had adopted the mindset of a life-long learner and sought mentorship in the areas of their weakness, they could have enjoyed their hard-earned 'spoils of war'.

Maybe you are the kind of person who walks through the office and doesn't connect with anyone, or is ready to bark orders at your employees but hopeless at knowing how to respond when they share their personal struggles with you. Interpersonal skills are vital for successful teamwork, and a lack of them will minimise your capacity to lead others.

Ultimately, your personality type, and natural strengths and weaknesses are not an excuse when it comes to the pursuit of success. The burden of leadership falls squarely on the leader to be what is needed for the team and for the organisation, so refusing to change is choosing to place limits around any potential success. Just as He has always been for me, the Holy Spirit is ready and able to place the spotlight on those areas in your life that need growth and development. All you have to do is ask Him and have the courage to follow through when He prompts.

Adding 'Super' to the 'Man'

I have made it my mission to grow and develop in critical areas of my weakness when it is in my power to do so. But there are some skills that are absent or weak that would require extraordinary amounts of time and energy to develop—'commodities' that are rare at this stage of my life. In these cases, when the cost of personal development outweighs the potential gains, I have learnt to *staff* my weaknesses so that the organisation does not suffer because of them. 'Staffing your weaknesses' means finding people who are strong in those areas to fill in the gaps and release you to focus on your strengths.

Great care must be taken in selecting new staff to complement the skills of existing team members. Employing people in haste can lead to long-term issues that add to the burden of a leader rather than alleviating it. But when the right person is found, it can be a game-changer for the organisation!

My current assistant, Joey, is an incredible example of 'staffing your weakness'. Administration, organisation and written language are some of my greatest weaknesses even though they are essential aspects of managing my frenetic work life. As I mentioned previously, I left school early to take on a carpentry apprenticeship—mostly because I was labelled 'not academic' by teachers who could not manage my emerging leadership gift. God had placed in me all of the gifts and talents required to fulfil my calling, and with it, great potential—but I still struggled in some of the practical applications of those gifts.

My assistant, Joey, who is truly brilliant in her own right, has brought a level of order to my life that has dramatically increased my productivity and creativity. From tasks as simple as managing my diary to as complex as drafting legal letters, she has enabled me to function at a higher level than would have ever been possible without her. While it is true that I could have trained to improve my skills in these areas, I have been instead freed up to lead at a higher level knowing that the details of my life are in trustworthy hands. The scaffolding she brings to my life has enabled me to operate in high places of perspective and to focus only on those things that I alone can achieve according to my God-given purpose.

'Staffing your weaknesses' not only has practical advantages but also significant financial ones. Delegating the lesser (for lack of a better word!) tasks to others on a lower pay grade, releases higher paid leaders to do what they are paid to do—to THINK.

When disentangled from daily menial tasks, a leader can then oversee the business from a higher vantage point and with clearer perspective.

When disentangled from daily menial tasks, a leader can then oversee the business from a higher vantage point and with clearer perspective, anticipating opportunities and challenges and planning for them in advance.

There is a clear distinction between those workers who are content with merely following instructions from above (a bit like a worker bee in a colony) and the 'big thinkers' and dreamers who revolutionise a business with a simple idea. Both are essential members of the team but have very different daily demands in the workplace. Knowing which employee is which and positioning them for maximum benefit within the organisation is the key to great success. An ideas person, for example, who lacks organisational skills, may just be the greatest asset to the business when complemented by the right team members who can offset their weakness.

Are you spending too much time and energy trying to resolve your weaknesses when you could be employing someone to fill the gap?

The Buck Stops Here

I once heard it said that leadership is both the problem and the solution—a thought that impacted me greatly as a young leader.

Blaming team members for an organisation's poor performance or failure to meet customer expectations is tempting but misguided. Almost always, an individual's failure to perform can be traced back to poor or inadequate leadership. Perhaps the expectations were not clear or the employee was not supervised properly or trained adequately. Maybe undealt-with conflict between team members had spilled out into the customer arena, or evidence of integrity breaches were swept 'under the carpet' so as not to offend or lose a gifted worker. Whatever the case may be, great leaders examine themselves and the role they have played in organisational failure before holding their staff to account.

As we have already discussed, leadership is both a privilege and responsibility that requires great humility. Taking personal responsibility for your role in any failure of the business, even if indirect, will endear any leader to their team and encourage openness, vulnerability and honesty in return.

In my role as a senior pastor, I would take care never to reactively chase down an individual staff member when complaints would inevitably be made about our services, sound levels, facilities etc. I learned to investigate my own role in the breakdown first so that when the time came to address the matter with team members, I could be as informed and gracious as possible. I found that this produced great relational returns and a staff who were loyal and transparent.

Do you have an employee problem? What is YOUR role in the issue?

The buck stops with you.

Attaining and Retaining Great Team Players

Then the Lord answered me and said:
"Write the vision and make it plain on tablets,
that he may run who reads it.

— *Habakkuk 2:2 (NKJV)*

I have learned first-hand that great vision attracts great people.

Some years ago, I remember standing before a group of business people sharing the vision for my church. I diverted for a few minutes to share a dream I had in my heart about advertising our church on television to attract the lost. At that time, this huge dream was completely out of reach, but I loved inspiring people with the future possibilities that God had planted in my heart.

When the event was over, a businessperson approached me and offered to pay for the initial commercials to get the vision in my heart up and running immediately. There were many other day-to-day expenses that I really needed help with, but this big—thinking, Kingdom-minded person was captivated by the bigger vision and wanted to invest in it. Up until that moment, he had never really given to the church consistently, or stepped up to meet any immediate needs, but here he saw an opportunity to be part of something great and jumped at it. I from this that vision has the power to switch on and activate big thinkers and great team members!

Celebrating the now-achievements of your business is important, but should always be coupled with a consistent declaration of future possibilities that keeps the team thinking ahead and constantly moving forward and upward. When big thinking, gifted and well-resourced individuals are attracted to the vision and added to the team, the potential of your business multiplies exponentially. Simply put, if you want to keep expanding your business, you must keep expanding your team—and if you want to keep expanding your team, you must keep casting big vision!

Having a clearly defined strategic plan or vision for your business is crucial in attracting and retaining great team players. The truth is, people are primarily drawn to vision—not money—and if they believe in that vision, they will stay on to become loyal and fruitful employees through both challenging and fruitful seasons. Where vision is unclear, team players are more likely to revert to the mindset of an employee—simply showing up to work and getting the immediate job done in order to take home a pay cheque, but having no vested interest in the long-term growth of the business. Employees tend to adhere strictly to their working conditions (working hours, leave entitlements etc.) and fail to offer the flexibility of fully-invested and satisfied team players.

Failure to provide a clear strategic plan for your team that is kept at the forefront of every activity, can result in great team players either leaving your organisation to follow a stronger vision elsewhere, or worse, creating and pursuing their own vision while still working for you. This effectively creates 'di-vision' within the team, with the responsibility falling squarely at the feet of the leader for failure to engage the team in the outworking of the vision.

Great leaders go beyond simply measuring results and progress based on the plan they have set for the team. This does not promote ownership of the vision and creates a 'success or fail' mindset without the space to develop leadership capacity. On the other hand, involving different team members in creating departmental plans that service the overall strategic plan promotes ownership and makes team members feel honoured, valuable and heard. Empowering team members to contribute to the vision breeds excitement and the motivation to achieve above and beyond the goals and expectations of the vision.

Empowering team members to contribute to the vision breeds excitement and the motivation to achieve the vision.

A clear vision and strategic plan today pre-determines tomorrow's results. Some have said that forward planning limits God's ability to speak to us and guide us in the moment, but I don't believe this to be true. I have found the opposite. Having a clear strategic plan with clearly defined goals, doesn't stop me from hearing God's voice and adjusting the vision accordingly. But until I hear specific direction from God, I choose to follow the blueprint He gave me at the start of my journey, knowing with confidence that He is always directing my path.

In all your ways acknowledge Him, and He shall direct your paths.

— Proverbs 3:6 (NKJV)

Planning to Win

As we have discussed, one of the greatest biblical characters and strategists was King David. In the account of his great wartime victories—found in 2 Samuel chapter 8—we see him slowly and strategically conquering army after army. He started with enemies that he knew his soldiers were capable of defeating before tackling more intimidating ones. This gave his soldiers a psychological advantage and instilled much needed courage and confidence in them for the more challenging battles that lay ahead. Over a 2-year period, he took an entire kingdom—battle by battle—not in a spontaneous, unplanned way, but by strictly adhering to a strategic plan and building confidence in his team as they moved forward towards the ultimate prize.

In a similar way to building an enterprise, David waited on God for clear direction before choosing locations where he could build strongholds that would later serve to defeat enemy armies in the moment of war. He formulated a plan and stuck to it until he took out the ultimate prize and shared the spoils of war with his team.

How we perform in the little battles is so important in preparing our teams for much larger ones where there is far more on the line. This may mean taking on smaller and more manageable projects in the beginning—to build confidence and skills—before attempting larger, more lucrative ventures that may fail on account of a team that is enthusiastic but inexperienced. Put another way, it is better to take on manageable projects and win—therefore building strength and confidence in your team and credibility in your leadership—than accepting larger challenges prematurely, losing ground and shattering the confidence of your team.

Do those on your team clearly understand the vision of your business and what it is that you are trying to achieve? Do you keep the vision at the forefront of their minds at all times? Are you building with employees who simply show up, do their job and go home, or passionate, engaged team members who are self-motivated to see the vision fulfilled?

Embracing Failure

Mistakes are inevitable because we are all human. The point is whether you make room for them and how you deal with them in your organisation.

I was that kid who always had to learn a lesson the hard way. Once as a young carpentry apprentice on a minimal wage—forced to do all of the 'dog jobs' on the building site—my boss walked past me and warned me not to chisel too close to a pane of glass in case I broke it. Full of adolescent self-confidence and not great at heeding advice, I, of course, chiselled too close to the glass, smashed it and experienced the very justified wrath of my boss. When he had finished blasting me, he made a statement that has left a lasting impact on me to this day:

"Hey Smithy, that's what we pay you for—to make mistakes. Just don't do it again."

I understand now that this is the very reason why apprentices are paid less than their qualified counterparts—to accommodate their inevitable failings!

Later, as a boss and leader myself, I made strategic decisions to plan for the mistakes that would be inevitably made by my teams. For example, I always factored in a 'damage budget' and watertight insurance policy for the youth staff of my church knowing that they lacked experience, wisdom and leadership skills, and often engaged in high-risk activities. By making room for future mistakes, the sting of those mistakes was removed and I was less inclined to blast them for it in the moment. It wasn't that I didn't bring appropriate correction and discipline when needed, but that I made room for these judgement lapses and ensured that the consequences—financial, relational, health etc.—were taken care of in advance so that the organisation would not suffer as a result. In the height of the moment, I was able to manage my irritation and frustration by adopting the mindset of my building site boss and extending grace to those who were in a learning phase.

Not only are mistakes to be expected as a normal part of life, but they are the catalyst to learning and growth in our teams.

There is an old English proverb which says, "He who makes no mistakes never makes anything." And I think it was James Joyce who said, "Mistakes are the portals of discovery."

The truth is, if you want to build an incredible team in your business, you must embrace making mistakes. Mistakes are the natural outcome of risk-taking and trying new things that **Mistakes are the natural** may launch the business into new levels of **outcome of risk-taking.** success.

Rarely do people mean to make a mistake, but how they are dealt with in response to those mistakes is crucial to the development of a great team.

One of the greatest tools a leader can use is his or her own personal stories about the mistakes they have made and what they learned as a result. When we learn to talk openly about our weaknesses and past mistakes with our teams, we empower them to admit to their own and seek the help they need to grow and develop beyond those mistakes. The alternative is team members who are so fearful of making mistakes that they stay within the 'safe zone' and never realise their full potential, or worse, cover up their mistakes and create vulnerability and risk for the business as a result.

As a leader, being vulnerable by owning our mistakes is powerful. Many years ago, I saw an opportunity for my church to acquire more space by leasing an adjoining building. I called the church to pray and bring a special offering to fund the lease. Full of faith, the people brought an unusually large and generous offering, and we were able to inhabit the space and expand our programs. Unfortunately, not long after, the building was sold by the owner and we were forced to vacate it. Naturally, the people were very discouraged—as was I.

The next time a need presented itself, I followed the exact same format, calling the church to pray and give so that we could purchase some equipment. I was incredibly disappointed when the offering taken was much less than the first. Realising that I had not asked God for a new strategy and instead mindlessly followed the same process I had previously for the lease, which later failed, I felt compelled to apologise to the church. I admitted to both the staff and to the church that I had followed a formula and not the will of God, and apologised for letting them down in my leadership.

Straight after confessing my error to the church, a couple walked up to me and explained that they had not given to the latest offering for equipment because they were unsure how they felt about the presentation I had made. They did not feel right in giving at that moment, but now felt released by God to give after hearing my honest confession and apology for my leadership mistake. They gave generously, not because they were overly committed to the need that was presented, but because my humility and integrity made them feel secure in my leadership and my ability to direct their giving to a worthwhile cause. By admitting my weakness, I had inadvertently built trust in this couple, and trust is one of the most valuable things a team member can give you.

As I have already mentioned, pride is our greatest enemy that will hold us back from admitting our mistakes and keep us working hard to present ourselves and our businesses as shining examples of perfection—a false reflection of truth that will eventually be exposed for what it is. Remember that admitting fault is not a weakness, but a great strength that breeds stability and security amongst team members. Paul dramatically emphasised this principle by claiming to 'boast' of his weaknesses so that God's enabling grace would be attracted to his circumstances.

SCAN & WATCH

But he said to me, "My grace is sufficient for you, for my power is made perfect in weakness." Therefore I will boast all the more gladly about my weaknesses, so that Christ's power may rest on me. That is why, for Christ's sake, I delight in weaknesses, in insults, in hardships, in persecutions, in difficulties. For when I am weak, then I am strong.

— *2 Corinthians 12:9-10 (NIV)*

Developing a culture where team members can safely admit weakness without fear of lasting consequence should be the priority of every great leader. It doesn't mean allowing weaknesses and errors to continue indefinitely without authentic growth and change, but it does encourage the Christlikeness in us to develop as we practice the kind of grace that we would like to be extended towards us when our own failures surface.

Developing a culture where team members can safely admit weakness should be the priority of every great leader.

The truth is, we ALL want to belong to a team where we feel secure and accepted—regardless of our natural strengths and weaknesses.

We all want to grow, develop and learn.

We all expect to be disciplined and corrected fairly when we fall short.

So are YOU embracing and making room for mistakes in your team?

The Spoils of War

One of the greatest mistakes a marketplace leader can make is to fail to appropriately acknowledge and celebrate the contribution of each team member—whether great or small.

When the armies of the Old Testament went to war, it was only those who fought in the battle as part of the collective army that were eligible to share the spoils of war that came with victory. This was a direct and tangible acknowledgement that any person who contributed was worthy of reward.

One of the worst decisions a leader can make is to assign the spoils of war to a favoured few at the top but fail to acknowledge the efforts of the rest of the team. The truth is, battles are not won by the leader alone—no matter how gifted he or she may be. As tempting as it may be, a leader should never take all of the credit for success without rightfully acknowledging the critical role that every team member played in the win. Each should be celebrated and rewarded if we want them to feel ownership for the vision. Having a 'that's what they're paid to do' mindset towards your team will keep them at a distance and less likely to bring their A-game at the moment when it counts.

Consider the attitude of a dictator for a moment. Motivated by insecurity and an unrelenting thirst for power that they are not entitled to, dictators tend to have a 'god complex' and seek accolades for themselves and not those around them. We can see this at work in King Saul when he was filled with jealousy at the success and bravery of one of his team members:

> *As they returned home, after David had killed the Philistine, the women poured out of all the villages of Israel singing and dancing, welcoming King Saul with tambourines, festive songs, and lutes. In playful frolic the women sang, Saul kills by the thousand, David by the ten thousand! This made Saul angry—very angry. He took it as a personal insult. He said, "They credit David with*

'ten thousands' and me with only 'thousands.' Before you know it they'll be giving him the kingdom!" From that moment on, Saul kept his eye on David.

— *1 Samuel 18:6-9 (MSG)*

In the first few years of his hugely successful business empire Microsoft, Bill Gates made a decision not to stockpile extreme wealth for himself alone, but to create opportunities for others to join him in building the company and in sharing the spoils of war. As a result, over a thousand people in his organisation went on to become millionaires themselves on account of Bill's willingness to embrace a team-approach to business.

When a leader fails to reward a team member fairly for their efforts, the opportunity is missed to build strength, security and loyalty within the team. Value judgements are subjective and human nature tends to want to reward the 'shooting stars' of the business while neglecting the relatively unseen, faithful workhorses who complete all of the mundane but essential tasks that keep the business operating from a position of strength. It isn't until we lose an employee like this— when they leave in search of a boss who values their efforts— that we realise the critical role they have played in winning battles. Shooting stars are entertaining to watch but quickly lose their light, while the unnoticed masses of smaller stars faithfully shine on, night after night!

Shooting stars are entertaining to watch but quickly lose their light, while the unnoticed masses of smaller stars faithfully shine on.

Are you communicating value to your entire team?

A Risk Worth Taking

Betrayal is one of the worst human experiences and its impact is directly proportional to the level of trust you extended to a person. It is my experience that betrayal in life is to be expected. People we trust will walk away. Those we have invested in will take that investment for granted and serve someone else. This may sound discouraging, but it does not have to be. When you are prepared for it and navigate it well in your team, it can become an opportunity for personal as well as team growth.

While I do not advocate that you lead with a constant expectation of being betrayed, I do encourage you to settle in your heart that it is likely to happen at some point to prepare yourself so that you and your business are not shipwrecked by the breach of integrity of someone you trusted. Most people do not set out to betray their leader or team, but simply succumb to self-interest when pressure is applied. Having said that, others ARE driven by self-interest and are by nature opportunistic in their outlook.

This is real life and it can make you withdraw from trusting anybody. However, the choice not to trust people is then a choice to keep your business small.

Trust is something that must be built over time and is proportionate to the time and energy we invest into building relationships with our team members. When we know people intimately, we are more sensitive to the signs that they are not doing well and have the opportunity to stop any divisive action before it begins. But if we keep our teams at arms length, building protective walls around ourselves and avoiding vulnerability and healthy conflict, we actually set ourselves up for betrayal.

Even Jesus understood and embraced the likelihood of betrayal. Despite knowing that Judas would lack integrity when it counted, He did not withhold His trust and grace, and continued to invest in the relationship knowing that His loyalty would never be reciprocated.

What I love about the story of Judas is that God used the most severe betrayal recorded in history to see His purposes achieved and His glory revealed. Betrayal—as horrible as it is— can still be used by God for good in our lives. As painful as my experiences of betrayal have been, I know that they have helped me grow and develop into a better leader and team player.

Trust is risky, but yields huge dividends when practised. We can choose to camp ourselves at betrayal points in our lives and focus all of our energy on ensuring that it never happens to us again, OR we can spend that same energy strengthening and deepening our relationships with our team members in the hope that they will stand the test of time and trial. The choice is ours.

There is nothing more frustrating and defeating than working for a boss or leading a team member whose M.O. is to refuse to trust you or let you penetrate the walls they have built as a result of past betrayal. On the other hand, remaining openhearted, authentic and vulnerable—though not naïve— encourages team members to do the same, and to move forward and upward together to see the vision accomplished.

Do you trust your team?

Who's at the Helm?

When it comes to selecting the team to surround us in our business, it is easy to look to trusted family members and friends to fill positions, instead of throwing the net out widely into less predictable waters.

It is natural to want to involve our children and family in our business endeavours, especially when we have built the business from the ground up and view it as our legacy. But limiting the pool of team members to family and friends can greatly limit the growth potential of the business.

Working with family and friends can be simple in some ways, but complicated in others. Where history and emotions are involved, the normal processes of business operation can become complex and interwoven. I can't tell you how many professionals I have known who have had the unenviable task of trying to demote, re-position or fire a friend or family member who is not performing or compromising the business in some way. When a deeper level of relationship is involved, the repercussions of conflict in the workplace can be severe.

While it is true that some businesses thrive when run by family members, these families are not usually the norm. The ability to emotionally separate work and home life, and to continue to honour and love each other despite work-related conflict, is a special and rare skill that evades most families.

Even in the ministry context, working with family is a complex business. While I have always been very careful not to communicate an unreasonable expectation that my children should choose the ministry when they are old enough, the truth is, I could think of no greater privilege than to work alongside them pursuing the call of God. Even the ministry is a 'family business' of sorts with the same temptations to keep the business in the family. But I have seen this devastate too many families when rigid expectation is involved.

My advice to professionals who secretly—or not so secretly—hope that their children and spouses will join the team and build the business alongside them, is to remind themselves who the business owner really is. Who is at the *helm* of your business?

Helm *noun* (Merriam-Webster dictionary)

1. a lever or wheel controlling the rudder of a ship for steering broadly; the entire apparatus for steering a ship
2. a position of control

As Christians, God should undisputedly be at the helm of our business, which is greatly comforting if we genuinely yield control and allow Him to lead. He knows who the ideal team members are and where they can be found. He knows who will stay for a while and who will stay for a lifetime. He knows the plans and the purposes He has for every individual person and for the business as a whole. He IS the ultimate CEO.

When you hold onto your business too tightly, you risk losing everything anyway.

When you hold onto your business too tightly, trying desperately to maintain control at all times so that your investment will not crumble, you risk losing everything anyway.

When I was a young and upcoming pastor, I learned a lot from an older man who served on our church's board at the time. He was a very accomplished man and highly respected, but had an issue with control. Whenever other board members differed in their opinions or presented ideas that differed from his personal vision for the church (not the pastor's), he would become aggressive and at times, manipulative. He struggled to cope with change but the church was moving forward, with or without him.

This man was a staunch believer in democracy and loved engaging in the politics of convincing others to vote in a certain way, using fear as the motivation. Many times, he was able to stop the pastor's vision from proceeding by ensuring that there were not enough votes to carry the motion, but this same democratic process one day caught up with him when he was voted off the board for constantly resisting progress and vision. As he left, another board member declared that if he insisted on living by the sword, he must also be prepared to die by it.

Although I greatly admired this man's faith and commitment to the church, I learned that these traits are of little value if you cannot let go of control when it is right to do so.

I remember hearing a story about a young apprentice who fell from a great height on the building site I was working on. Paralysed by fear, he gripped onto the scaffolding as he fell and hung suspended in the air until emergency services arrived. Even when a platform was raised under him and he was no longer at risk of falling to his death, he was unable to voluntarily let go off the scaffolding so they could help him. In the end, they had to break his fingers with a piece of wood, adding significant injury to his trauma, just to release his grip!

I wonder how many businesses lose momentum and eventually fail because the owner or director simply could not let go of control and allow God to steer the ship into new and uncharted waters. When we see God as the head of our businesses, we can operate with the confidence that He has a plan that surpasses our natural understanding and will ensure that we find the right team to implement the vision He placed in our hearts. But when we refuse to loosen our grip of the wheel, we risk never sailing beyond the perceived safety of the harbour.

Who is at the helm of your business?

Acknowledging Your Limits

I love the story of Moses. Chosen and positioned by God to fulfil the extraordinary mandate of leading His people out of the captivity of Egypt and into the Promised Land, Moses was faced with the overwhelming task of governing and leading an entire nation on his own.

Having been strategically placed in the palaces of Egypt as a child, God had allowed Moses to be trained in how to govern a nation, yet he still could not do it alone. Exhausted and struggling to keep up with the needs of the multitudes, while neglecting his own needs and that of his family, he was rebuked by his father-in-law who could see that he was self-destructing in his leadership.

> *Moses' father-in-law replied, 'What you are doing is not good. You and these people who come to you will only wear yourselves out. The work is too heavy for you; you cannot handle it alone.'*
> — *Exodus 18:17-18 (NIV)*

He wisely listened to Jethro's advice and appointed a team of people to help him— positioning them over 10s, 50s, 100s and 1000s of people, according to their ability. Moses trained and discipled them, and they in turn ran the business on his behalf within their own sphere of influence. In this way, God's people were cared for and Moses was freed up to lead at a higher level and live a healthier, more balanced life.

It is often very difficult to admit that we need help and even harder to trust others to do what we believe only we can do well.

Many of us believe, even insist, that we can do everything ourselves and do not need any help—that we are indispensable and unbreakable. But many have discovered, like me, that this is simply not true. It is often very difficult to admit that we need help and even harder to trust others to do what we believe only we can do well. Moses' story teaches us that God approves of delegation, often making the tasks He sets before us impossible without it.

Even though highly skilled, trained, called, appointed and anointed for the task, Moses could not fulfil his God-given purpose on his own. God and His Kingdom are all about TEAM. We are not called to complete the vision He places in our hearts alone. He has a team of people who He has been preparing for years, waiting to surround you and help see the vision fulfilled.

Are you struggling to let go and make space for others to rise in your organisation?

Examine the Roots

I'd like to finish this discussion on building a winning team by challenging you to look a little deeper—beyond the surface—to what lies at the root of your motivation to build a great team around you.

The older I have grown, the more aware I am of the generations running behind me. It only feels like yesterday that I was one of them, surging ahead in the prime of my life—full of vision and dreaming big. I felt invincible and life was full of possibilities. Although I still believe that the best lies ahead for me, I am now acutely aware that it is already time to turn my attention to the next generation and champion THEM to live fruitful lives for the Kingdom of God.

Unfortunately, so many people enter the latter seasons of their lives still holding on to old ways of doing things and never really trusting the next generation to carry the baton and finish the race. It can be hard to accept the rapid technological changes happening in the world and even harder to speak the language of the new generation of potential team players in our organisations. When we have built a business from the ground up, it can be like our 'child'—not easily entrusted in the care of those we believe to be inexperienced.

When John the Baptist saw Jesus approaching him and realised that He was the 'One' he had been waiting for, he made a difficult but incredibly humble statement.

He must increase, but I must decrease.

— *John 3:30 (NKJV)*

He was secure enough to recognise when it was his time to shine, and when to step back and allow others to take the spotlight.

This principle is crucial in building a great team in your business.

Watching the upcoming generation shine, even outdoing my accomplishments at a much younger age, has become one of the greatest joys of my life. In some areas of my calling, I have already begun the process of decreasing in order to allow others to increase. It wasn't easy to admit that the moment had arrived, but it is so rewarding on the other side of that decision to let go. I consider it a great privilege to help others reach their full potential and become all that God has called them to become. In a strange way, their achievements become my achievements as I share in the joy of their fruitfulness and victories.

I love to disciple my team members, not only in work-related skills, but in life skills also. I genuinely want to see them thrive and achieve far above anything I dreamed for myself. Yes, the time to decrease came much sooner than I expected, but life is short and we must embrace and enjoy every season that God brings us to and through. I have learned that the greatest fruitfulness in my life is not always my own achievements, but the achievements of others whose lives I was entrusted by God to steward and develop.

> **I have learned that the greatest fruitfulness in my life is the achievements of others whose lives I was entrusted by God to steward and develop.**

So I challenge you to look at your teams in a different light. Are they just workers you have hired to do a job and bring in money, or are they people God has entrusted to you to develop, grow and draw out fruitfulness? Do you genuinely care about them? Do you take pleasure in watching them grow and mature? Are you willing to decrease in order to make room for others to step into the spotlight? Are you willing to embrace NEW ways of thinking and NEW methods of doing business, even when you have achieved success with the old?

I leave you with an Old Testament image that I hope will stay with you in your journey of team—building.

Shortly after their exodus from Egypt, God instructed His people to ensure that Hebrew slaves should not remain bound in service indefinitely, but that after six years, they should be given a free-will choice to leave their master or serve them forever. The choice to remain in service would result in a permanent mark to indicate their voluntary commitment.

> *But if the servant declares, 'I love my master and my wife and children and do not want to go free,' then his master must take him before the judges. He shall take him to the door or the doorpost and pierce his ear with an awl. Then he will be his servant for life.*
>
> *— Exodus 21:5-6 (NIV)*

To me, this speaks about those who sit under our leadership transitioning from serving us out of *obligation* to serving us out of *loyalty* and *love*. It should be our desire that those we work with are bonded with us in ways that far surpass the transactional nature of working for a wage. But just as it is their choice, so too it is our choice as leaders whether or not we will build our teams in a way that promotes longevity of service and a culture of mutual honour.

Perhaps one of the greatest testimonies of our marketplace ministry is the way that we select and treat those who serve alongside us in our God-given mandate.

Perhaps one of the greatest testimonies of our marketplace ministry is the way that we select and treat those who serve alongside us in our God-given mandate.

What is at the root of your motivation to build a great team?

Ultimately, it should be LOVE.

SHIFT

Having challenged you to think beyond the confines of your current measure of success and to begin viewing your life and business from the perspective of a king—called and anointed to minister in the marketplace—it is safe to say that the ball is well and truly 'in your court'. No one can force you to change or put in the disciplined effort required to alter your thinking and behaviour. What you do with what has been presented is entirely up to you.

I'm sure that some of you are content with the level of marketplace success you have achieved to date and I wish you well in the future. But others of you, like me, dream of *more*—more success, more resources, more influence, more faith and more impact for the Kingdom of God. Still others of you are just beginning the journey of marketplace ministry, full of vision and hope for your future. Wherever you are at right now, let me challenge you with this one thought: Are you operating in the position you were created for?

If the answer is "No", or you are unsure, maybe it's time for change.

If you desire to see change in the trajectory of your life and business, you MUST change the way you are currently *thinking* before you consider changing the things that you are *doing*. Real, lasting change is the result of transformed thinking and this will take time and focus to achieve—especially if you have been 'in the business' for some time. For some, however, changing your mind can be an instantaneous matter with accelerated results. No matter how long the process takes, your decision to SHIFT in your thinking will act as a powerful, unseen rudder that works to change the course of your endeavours, leading you to your unique, God-given destiny. Alternatively, failure to make the decision to change—when change is required—will see your ship continue on the same course, unchallenged indefinitely.

I need to take this moment to address one of the greatest limiting obstacles to thinking that I have encountered in the life of marketplace professionals to date. Michael E. Gerber's book, The E Myth, highlighted this to me many years ago and I have never forgotten it:

> *"...knowing how to do the work of a business has nothing to do with building a business that works."*
> — *Michael E. Gerber, The E Myth*

There are plenty of people who know how to do the work of a business and do it very well—excellent carpenters, competent accountants, brilliant architects and gifted baristas—just to name a few professions who may decide to try their hand at creating enterprises that capitalise on their talent, creativity and success. Usually these individuals are highly skilled, even outstanding in their field, and logically speaking, it makes sense to move from making profits for someone else to working for themselves. It is estimated that between 90% and 95% of all owner-operators fall into this category, building enterprises around their unique gift or talent or their work. However, the long-term success of these endeavours is very unpredictable and many do not survive or yield sizable profits. The remaining 5%-10% actually go on to build enterprises that work, but do not revolve around their work.

Confused? Let me explain.

Don't assume that because you are skilled in a craft of some sort, you will be successful in building an expansive venture around that craft. In fact, in my experience, sometimes too much knowledge, expertise and personal perfectionism can hinder expansion. Make no mistake— God honours people who master their gifts and talents, and opportunities follow those who are skilled. But when it comes to multiplying your

Sometimes too much knowledge, expertise and personal perfectionism can hinder expansion.

talents, getting caught up in the fine details of the operation can and will distract you from growing and taking your place as a king in the marketplace.

Unless a king quickly learns how to trust his team, delegate responsibility and empower others to operate within the scope of their unique gifts and talents, the progress and advancement of his kingdom will quickly grind to a halt as the weight of responsibility on his shoulders becomes unbearable.

The majority of people who seek to build a successful enterprise start their journey with an owner-operator mindset. While building anything from scratch is an admirable pursuit, I am talking to kings now! You were born for levels of significance, influence and dominion that extend far beyond the dream of owning a small business in isolation. I hope you will begin to imagine possibilities that press past the boundaries of your current thinking, moving beyond the limited mindset of an owner-operator to that of an *entrepreneur.*

An owner-operator begins as a skilled technician of some sort, and builds their enterprise around themselves. What they build reflects their own unique interests, disposition, dreams and skillset. That is why creating their own business is so attractive—because it reflects THEM. Time and energy is invested into working hard and creating a product that they are proud of and reflects their ethos and culture. They are self-employed and have control over the time they invest, which is a very attractive concept for anyone. However, if we look closely at what is really going on, we often find the owner-operator working many more hours than they once did, not necessarily making more money than the salary they once earned, and without a doubt, laying their head on the pillow at night weighed down by exponentially increasing worry and pressure. Ultimately, if the enterprise they so passionately set out to build fails, they will pay a high price. This is a reality that all owner-operators come face to face with shortly after their journey begins.

For some—many in fact—the idea of earning a salary that is consistent and worry-free, even if less profitable, becomes very attractive once again. In an attempt to put the failure behind them, they sell up their enterprise and return to the perceived 'greener pastures' of working for someone else.

If and when the owner-operator decides to sell up, they end up selling what they first purchased: they bought a job and they sold a job. They may have employees but because they are intrinsically involved in everyday operations, their enterprise remains relatively small during its lifetime and at best, turns over a reasonable profit and maintains itself. Sadly, in the end, many are sold at a loss. The most that many owner-operators can show for their huge investment of time, energy and emotion, is a reasonable income earned, a feeling of independence and the few assets that have been acquired along the way.

I don't believe that this is God's best for your life and this outcome is NOT in keeping with the inherited dominion that God has prepared for you as a king in the marketplace!

So what is the alternative?

Let's talk about the entrepreneurial mindset in contrast to the owner-operator mindset. Please don't get caught up with the terminology I am using. My hope is that you will draw out the truth and spit out the bones that come with the terminology.

So what does it mean to be an entrepreneur?

When I talk about entrepreneurs, I am referring to people who have innovative ideas that drive them to find ways to fill a void in the marketplace. They tend to be creative, passionate, productive and ambitious in their outlook.

In his book, the E-Myth, Michael E. Gerber put it this way:

> **"The entrepreneur builds an enterprise that liberates [him or] her, creates endless amounts of energy and increases their financial, emotional and mental capital exponentially. In the end, there is significant equity to show for [their] investment. The enterprise runs itself in the hands of professional management. It has real value in the world. The entrepreneur is now free to invest what [they have] learned in another enterprise...expand [their] reach and... add value to other people...all the while creating income that [he or] she no longer has to work for."**

What a contrast to the picture that the owner-operator paints. For many of us, the idea of investing in people and improving their lives is an integral part of our Christian ethos and we want so much more for our employees than simply making 'ends meet'. But if we are struggling to produce increased resources in our own lives, how can we improve the lives of others? It is from a place of personal abundance that a king is positioned to improve the lives of others. We are called to be conduits of provision and favour. This is both the responsibility and privilege of being a king and should compel us to break out of owner-operator thinking, and instead study and imitate the mindset of the entrepreneurial thinker!

It is from a place of personal abundance that a king is positioned to improve the lives of others.

Having said that, it is possible for the pendulum to swing too far in the opposite direction. If ALL we are focussed on is creating income that we no longer have to work for, then we have drifted away from a true Kingdom mindset. I work in the ministry and have a strong work ethic. Although the years are flying by, I am not working for the purpose of retirement. So many people I know *work* hard so that they can eventually *play* hard, but our personal comfort is not the high calling to which we have been called. I love personal comfort as much as the next person, but it is not my primary pursuit.

> **But seek first his kingdom and his righteousness, and all these things will be given to you as well.**
> — *Matthew 6:33 (NIV)*

I am certainly focussed on making myself redundant in the areas I have been entrusted to govern, but not so that I can work less. I ease myself out of every leadership structure when the time is right, so that I can refocus my energy elsewhere and continue expanding the Kingdom of God with my gifts and talents. By getting out of the way, I make room for others to rise up and realise their dreams, and this brings me enormous pleasure. I am not looking for an easy life but to continue investing my skills wherever I can to see increase for the Kingdom of God. While this remains my focus, I can also trust that God will meet my personal needs and build MY house, rewarding me with opportunities to relax and rejuvenate throughout the journey.

Both the owner-operator and the entrepreneur have the same amount of time to invest, but the latter receives a superior return. It is up to you which path you take. Make no mistake; if you have been operating in a limited capacity and are beginning to feel a stirring to believe for more, you will need to take time out to examine your thinking right down to the core beliefs that form the foundation of that thinking. Were you taught by a parent or mentored by a certain boss to think the way you do? Do you lack the personal confidence to believe that you can be more? Do you believe that you must be in the trenches with your employees at all times to be respected? These and many questions and many more need to be asked and answered honestly if you wish to make a shift to thinking like a king.

I'm aware that those of you who are reading this book will be at different stages of your journey. Some will be currently employed by others; some working as contractors, consultants or technicians; and still others of you will have reached the point of becoming owner-operators of your own enterprises. Whatever position you find yourself in now, it's time to explore new possibilities.

Consider how you might leverage your time to create more income than you currently do. Here is a simple key to get you started: Don't continue to engage for the long term in tasks that someone else can do just as well. Consider employing people to do these things so that you can be released to do what no one else can. This is the sweet spot of your unique calling, the place where you feel most energised and creative, and not anchored down with mundane everyday tasks that yield very few motivational returns. Consider how you can elevate someone else by moving out of the way and making space for them to rise to new levels of responsibility. After all, there is nothing worse than working for someone who hogs all of the creative real estate and banishes others to the often joyless task of putting legs on their boss' dreams, while never finding expression of their own. You will never know what true greatness lies dormant in your team members until you give them the opportunity to rise. That will mean getting out of the way, which is going to take some FAITH—faith in others, faith in yourself and above all, faith in a God who wants to take you higher and further than you ever thought possible!

A word of caution—I am not suggesting that you drop everything overnight and make radical, careless decisions that endanger your future unnecessarily. Our thinking usually doesn't change overnight and neither should we. Take your time and do things right. Consult God at every point of a decision and take people on a journey with you.

Let me use a simple example of this principle from my own life. When my children were very young, my wife took maternity leave from her work in our church to care for them before gradually integrating back into working at a greater capacity. During the process, we had to consider certain factors in our decision-making: what household tasks could be delegated to others to release her to pursue her calling in the ministry, and what tasks could she, and only she, do.

For me, it was simple. If she was to return to the family business (for us—the ministry), we would need to employ a cleaner and ironing lady at a minimum. Mothering the children, however, was not a task that anyone could do but her, and cooking was also a borderline issue. In my opinion, no one could understand and respond to the particular tastes of her family like she could. So, the obvious answer was that she should return to work when the kids were old enough to attend day care, but minimise her hours so that she could be the familiar face at the door to collect them, spend quality time with them in the afternoon and cook dinner for the family. And so the decision was made.

However, Leonie struggled with the idea of outsourcing the cleaning and ironing, having been raised in a home where her mother worked full time AND tended to the entire household duties as well. She could not reconcile the idea of paying someone to do what she was perfectly capable of doing herself. She had watched her mum work her fingers to the bone for the family and formed the core belief that real love could only be expressed through hard work. As a result, she continued to juggle BOTH work and home duties, and predictably, her creativity, passion and energy all suffered as a result. She eventually surrendered to outsourcing the domestic duties which then released her to focus on her unique calling—the things that brought her great joy and led to increased fruitfulness and productivity.

You will never enter the true zone of your creative potential while you remain chained to everyday tasks that someone else could be doing.

I know this is a simple, domestic example, but I hope you caught the gist of what I am trying to communicate. You will never enter the true zone of your creative potential while you remain chained to everyday tasks that someone else could be doing. This might be hard for you to hear, but YOU may well be your biggest problem. YOU may be the reason that your dreams are not coming to pass. YOUR mindset and behaviours may well be the reason your business is stunted and may never become all that you hoped it would. The problem lies with YOU, but then so does the solution!

I divert for a moment to address those of you who may be offended by what I am suggesting here—fully content with working hard to build a small but strong enterprise in which you are fully involved on a day-to-day basis. If that's you, I truly commend you on your work ethic and contentment, but can I take you to God's Word for a moment?

The Parable of the Talents in Matthew 25 is a well-known passage. Jesus tells the story of a man who entrusted five talents to one of his servants, two to another and one to a third servant. The man went on a trip and upon his return, assessed how each servant had fared with his share of talents.

> *So he who had received five talents came and brought five other talents, saying, "Lord, you delivered to me five talents; look, I have gained five more talents besides them." His lord said to him, "Well done, good and faithful servant; you were faithful over a few things, I will make you ruler over many things. Enter into the joy of your lord." He also who had received two talents came and said, "Lord, you delivered to me two talents; look, I have gained two more talents besides them." His lord said to*

him, "Well done, good and faithful servant; you have been faithful over a few things, I will make you ruler over many things. Enter into the joy of your lord."

Then he who had received the one talent came and said, "Lord, I knew you to be a hard man, reaping where you have not sown, and gathering where you have not scattered seed. And I was afraid, and went and hid your talent in the ground. Look, there you have what is yours."

But his lord answered and said to him, 'You wicked and lazy servant, you knew that I reap where I have not sown, and gather where I have not scattered seed. So you ought to have deposited my money with the bankers, and at my coming I would have received back my own with interest. So take the talent from him, and give it to him who has ten talents.

— Matthew 25:20-28 (NKJV)

As Christians, we all want to hear God say, "Well done, good and faithful servant" when we meet Him face to face. So who in this parable did God consider to be good and faithful? Was it the man who simply maintained what he had in his hand? The answer is obvious. In the context of this parable, Jesus was strongly expressing His displeasure at the maintenance mindset that drove one man to hide what he had been given while others were busy seeking increase and expansion. It is interesting to note that the root of this decision was FEAR (See verse 25). Fear is often hidden under the guise of common sense and practicality, but it is no less destructive in its quest to shut down God-given destiny and purpose in our lives.

The message here cannot be mistaken. God EXPECTS increase in our lives, and He expects us to multiply the gifts He has given us. Maintaining ground does not please Him, perhaps because it is not reflective of

His nature. In every living thing He created, He placed the potential for multiplication. In fact, one of His very first commandments to mankind, reflected this very desire in His heart:

> *Then God blessed them, and God said to them, "Be fruitful and multiply; fill the earth and subdue it; have dominion over the fish of the sea, over the birds of the air, and over every living thing that moves on the earth."*
> *— Genesis 1:28 (NKJV)*

Notice His order: blessing—fruitfulness—multiplication—subjection — dominion.

The one who buried his talent in the ground and maintained what was given, did not even progress beyond stage 1: the blessing phase. The reality is that we too, as marketplace ministers, have a responsibility to move through the stages and reach for the ultimate goal of *dominion*, just as the Father commanded from creation.

Dominion *noun*
/dəˈmɪnjən/

1. sovereignty or control.
2. the territory of a sovereign or government.

We once again find ourselves thinking in the realm of royalty. But I can sense your lack of self-belief! No need for insecurity. God's calling is always accompanied by His empowerment so if we are going to step into a higher realm of operation in every area of our lives, we must seek His anointing—the mark or seal that sets us apart for divine use, empowers us to accomplish God's work and protects us on the journey.

I want to take this moment to reassure you that stepping up to present yourself to be used by God for Kingdom exploits does not mean that you are saying "yes" to working even harder than you already do! This is a common little thought that enters the mind of many who are already busy and often weary believers, at the very moment when they consider responding to God's call to step up to a new level. When entertained, it can become a comfortable foothold for the enemy to enter the arena and yield influence on your decision—and it is never with your good in mind!

But I'm sure you know what to do.

> *For the weapons of our warfare are not carnal but mighty in God for pulling down strongholds, casting down arguments and every high thing that exalts itself against the knowledge of God, bringing every thought into captivity to the obedience of Christ...*
> — *2 Corinthians 10:4-5 (NKJV)*

Instead of working *harder*, this is a call to work *smarter* with what you have been given—but this may take some restructuring of your current mindsets about your working life (and in fact, every other area of your life). The truth is that everyone has the same number of hours to work with, but some use their time more effectively than others.

Everyone has the same number of hours to work with, but some use their time more effectively than others.

Instead of approaching this mindset shift with the question, "How much more will be required of me?", the better and for some, more challenging question may in fact be, "What am I prepared to let go of?" This is especially true of those of us who receive affirmation and identity from what we do.

The hardest thing I have had to learn to do in my work is letting go of *tangible* responsibilities to pursue *intangible* possibilities and opportunities. The main reason is because, like most of you, I like to be in control, and letting go means empowering others to take authority and embracing the very real possibility that they will do a substandard job. However, I am beginning to realise that most end up actually doing a better job than I could have done myself!

I have learned to be content, even thrive, in an environment where the people I have empowered to do what I once did, report to me once a week with a run-down of how things are progressing. Having slowly rid myself of the impulsive need to step in and correct them continuously, I am now free to listen without judgement and give thought to some of their innovative ideas. The reality is, I am no less knowledgeable about the detailed happenings of my departments, yet I have been freed up to step back and look at things from a different perspective, anticipating problems before they happen and perceiving opportunities I might have once overlooked due to the distraction of busyness. As my team races around at the frenetic pace I once did myself, they often fail to see the solutions that are so readily obvious to me from my detached and 'elevated' perspective.

On the other hand, there are the odd days when I feel a little redundant. Problems and challenges sometimes never get as far as my office because those who work under me are competent and capable individuals. On these days, I am left with the uncomfortable question—What do I do now?—but this feeling only lasts as long as it takes the next great game-changing idea to float through my consciousness and reactivate my passion and energy for higher Kingdom purpose!

"The technician goes to work IN his business, the entrepreneur goes to work ON his business"
— *Michael E. Gerber, The E Myth*

At the end of the day, I am living in the revelation that everything I do has Kingdom purpose and, as such, will succeed. So when the inevitable happens and one of the people I delegate authority to fails monumentally, I rest in the assurance that God will sort it out. It's not about failing due diligence by abdicating my responsibilities, but instead delegating those that can be done by others so that I can be released to step up in my kingship and continue to multiply and increase the talents God has entrusted to me.

I understand that letting go of things that we have invested so much into is often accompanied by fear. Can I trust someone to care as much about my affairs as I do and conduct themselves in a way that represents me? But like every area of life, when fear surfaces, it is an indication that we need to spend more time with God and re-establish our trust in HIM and His good intentions for our lives.

When fear surfaces, it is an indication that we need to spend more time with God and re-establish our trust in HIM.

> *For I know the plans I have for you," declares the Lord, "plans to prosper you and not to harm you, plans to give you hope and a future.*
>
> *— Jeremiah 29:11 (NIV)*

Fear is a powerful but defeated foe. If allowed to rule in our lives, we will certainly never grow into the full potential that God had called us to. So what are you afraid of? What are you holding onto that you need to release to others?

I love reading about the journeys of highly successful business people and Gerber writes about one in particular that really captured my attention and challenged my thinking. It was the story behind the massively successful Walmart chain.

Walmart Inc. is an American multinational retail corporation that operates a chain of hypermarkets, discount department stores and grocery stores. The company was founded by Sam Walton in 1962 and is one of the highest grossing companies in the US. He started the company with the simple concept of offering low price merchandise with great service. 'Saving people money so they can live better' remains the driving vision of the company to this day.

Sam credited the rapid growth of Walmart not only to the low costs for his customers, but also to the fruitfulness of his partnerships. He relied on his associates to give customers the kind of shopping experience that would attract them back to the store. Sam shared his vision for the company with associates in a way that was nearly unheard of in the industry and made them partners in the success of the company. He firmly believed that these partnerships made Walmart the success it is.

The Walton family went on to become the richest family in America, with annual sales in the nearly 12,000 stores worldwide, yielding US$500 billion (as at 2018). The combined wealth of Sam's descendants is said to be in excess of US$162 billion to this day!

A second story that really challenged me to the core was a story of a businesswoman who started her own business on the very same day and in the same city as Walmart was launched. A lady by the name of Peggy, founded *Peggy's Diner*. Many years down the track, Peggy had to sell her diner due to ill health and sold it for a loss. Sam Walton, on the other hand, is known to have gone on to own a variety of corporations, and even an island in the Mediterranean somewhere. Up until his death in 1992, his net worth was recorded as US$8.6 billion!

During his latter years of life, I guarantee that Sam was not worrying about the details of how his corporations were being run or whether or not they would suffer while he was absent, holidaying on his own private island. No, I'm certain that he was living his life free of everyday working pressures, enjoying the luxuries that his big thinking provided, looking for ways to give generously to the needy and above all, watching his children and grandchildren become heirs of his fortune...which brings us back to poor Peggy.

It is reported that Peggy got up early every day to work at the diner. She worked hard to deliver good quality food and great service to her customers—cooking, doing dishes and serving at the register. She was a technician of sorts, great at what she did, but unable to grow beyond being the owner-operator of a small local business.

This striking contrast between the success of two people with a great idea and big ambition should teach us a lesson in our own lives as marketplace ministers today. Both used their gifts and talents throughout their lifetimes, but which one lived in such a way as to leave a significant footprint on Earth? Which became an influential voice in the marketplace and raised enough income to significantly impact the lives of many in need? Which one fulfilled their dream to not only provide for their own family, but to position them for ongoing influence during their own lifetimes?

It's a sad story, but one we do not need to replicate. We have seen in scripture that expansion and increase is not only desirable, but also expected as a king operating in the Kingdom of God. Anything less is to waste the precious time we have been given on Earth. Jesus used very strong words to describe God's reaction to a maintenance mindset in the parable of the talents:

> *For to everyone who has, more will be given, and he will have abundance; but from him who does not have, even what he has will be taken away. And cast the unprofitable servant into the outer darkness. There will be weeping and gnashing of teeth.*
>
> *— Matthew 25:29-30 (NKJV)*

I believe that one of the most significant obstacles to living a life that ultimately pleases our Creator is an inaccurate definition of *faithfulness*. If we are honest, most of us reduce the concept of faithfulness to 'showing up', 'loyalty', 'trustworthiness', 'dependability' and 'looking after' the things we have been entrusted with by God and man. Naturally, we admire and celebrate these attributes, though rarely are these the people through which God's Kingdom is radically established on Earth. While these definitions of faithfulness are all true, they do not accurately reflect the fullness of what the Parable of the Talents is really trying to tell us.

Twice in the parable, the master is recorded as saying, "Well done, good and faithful servant" (Matthew 25:21-23)—both times as a direct response to INCREASE or EXPANSION of the talents he had entrusted to his servants. Clearly, God's definition of faithfulness undeniably involves increase and expansion of the things that He has entrusted to us—not just loving care and maintenance.

God's definition of faithfulness undeniably involves increase and expansion of the things that He has entrusted to us—not just loving care and maintenance.

A *good* king maintains the kingdom well during the time of his reign, but a *great* king leaves a legacy far greater than the one that was gifted to him. The confronting and humbling truth is that God has invested in each one of us and expects a good return for that investment.

I am not trying to scare or guilt you into changing your ways, but simply to urge you to understand the gravity and potential of your call to marketplace ministry. Many young people raise their hands in excitement at business events I run, committing themselves to becoming someone of influence for the Kingdom of God. Who wouldn't want the thrill of the chase and the alluring promise of wealth and significance? While I love to see their passion and enthusiasm, I want them to understand that this is not a call to mediocrity and that dreaming of owning a small enterprise is not dreaming high enough! God has so much more for those who are willing to examine the limitations of their thinking and step outside of its comfortable boundaries.

To God, faithfulness and fruitfulness go hand in hand. True faithfulness means believing by faith to see increase in the raw materials you have been gifted with—not by working *harder*—but instead by working *smarter* and under the daily guidance of the Holy Spirit.

So I'm calling those of you who want to step into your rightful kingship; those of you who want to stand alongside other like-minded businesspeople and truly make an impact on the planet for the glory of God. I'm calling on those who can push past their insecurities, limiting mindsets and any offence you may be feeling at the strength of my challenge to you.

SCAN & WATCH

It's time to go to work ON your business and be released into the great exploits that await!

LEGACY

Recently I turned 50.

In the years leading up to this significant milestone, I found my focus shifting from my own personal ambition and driving pursuit of success to those of younger men and women—most significantly, my own children—and what I could do to set them up to win in life and faith. Of course, like every father, I have always wanted to leave my children in a great position financially when I'm gone. I would love my financial ceiling to be their floor, with the blessings I received in my lifetime reaching through the generations to continue prospering my grandchildren and great grandchildren beyond.

> **A good man leaves an inheritance to his children's children.**
> — *Proverbs 13:22 (AMP)*

When Reality Hits

This is a very godly, noble pursuit, but I believe that our legacy goes way beyond leaving a financial inheritance and is more about what we *impart* to the next generation than what we physically leave behind. In other words, it's less about what we leave FOR people and more about what we leave IN people. I believe that this kind of thinking is not just the result of waking up one day, feeling the aches and pains of aging and suddenly having the unpleasant revelation of what James was trying to say when he casually described our lives as being like a *mist*:

> **Why, you do not even know what will happen tomorrow. What is your life? You are a mist that appears for a little while and then vanishes.**
> — *James 4:14 (NIV)*

Although this certainly happened to me as mid-life approached, I believe that we inherit this kind of thinking from our Creator—the One in whose image we are made. You don't need to look far in the Bible to see that He was and continues to be constantly thinking and planning generationally, being unrestrained by time and space. His M.O. was and is to make generational promises (covenants) and keep them—proving Himself to be a faithful and trustworthy Father generation after generation.

> *Blessed are those who fear the Lord,*
> *who find great delight in his commands.*
> *Their children will be mighty in the land;*
> *the generation of the upright will be blessed.*
> *Wealth and riches are in their houses,*
> *and their righteousness endures forever.*
> *— Psalm 112:1-3 (NIV)*

The truth is, God has a plan of redemption for mankind and we play just one small part in that plan. What matters is that we step up to fulfil our unique role in the brief moment we so casually call our life.

Beyond Wealth

It is tempting to judge our success by the material possessions we have acquired along the way and can leave to the next generation, but this is very limiting thinking when it comes to our legacy. What we so often fail to consider is the immeasurable value of the wisdom we impart into others, enabling them to bear fruit in their lives. When we impart our wisdom and experience, we leave a deposit that empowers them to fulfil their own God-given destiny. These deposits prepare them for whatever may come in life, and can be transferred from generation to generation indefinitely.

As I have mentioned over the course of this book, one of the most successful leaders in the Bible was King David whose reign went on for over 400 years—well beyond the time of his death. Although he was extremely wealthy and undoubtedly left a fortune to his descendants, he left so much more that was difficult to quantify. He left systems, culture, values and resources that enabled the next generation to continue his work and their own long after he was gone.

Just like everything we have been discussing in this book, *legacy* does not just happen by chance. It is something we all must plan and prepare for, intentionally taking time out from the demands of our everyday lives to consider how we might impact the next generation now and after we have gone. Most of us get so caught up in the **The truth is that a great** 'here and now' that we rarely think about this **legacy begins right now.** at all. Some believe that legacy is something to think about later in life and too many finish their lives without leaving one at all. But the truth is that a great legacy begins right now.

The key question is this: What sort of impact do you want to make in your lifetime?

Do you want to achieve the kind of success that will bring you joy and comfort in your lifetime but fade away with you, or do you want the impact of your life to carry on through the lives of those who come after you?

If you want your life to leave a permanent imprint, the time to act is NOW.

Stepping Back to Make Room

Jesus Himself left an incredible legacy that continues to affect the world profoundly, thousands of years later. Throughout His very short, yet powerful and influential life, we see Him intentionally communicating, teaching and imparting godly wisdom into the lives of a small number of disciples (followers/pupils) and practically demonstrating the Kingdom of God in their presence. As they did life together, Jesus seized every opportunity He could to equip them with what they would need to live fruitful lives and continue His work after His death. He did this by building an environment of trusting RELATIONSHIP.

Jesus used every opportunity available to teach His disciples how to advance Heaven's cause in the present. Yet at the same time, He never lost sight of the bigger picture—the long game of God's eternal Kingdom. Similarly, if we want to leave a lasting legacy, we must learn to harness the 'now opportunities' for Kingdom endeavour, while at the same time teaching those that we lead to have an eternal perspective.

Jesus approached the process of imparting into and discipling those entrusted to Him in a very simple but effective way:

1. He identified potential disciples and invited them to walk alongside Him and observe as He modelled the Kingdom of God in operation.

> *Then He said to them, "Follow Me, and I will make you fishers of men." They immediately left their nets and followed Him.*
> — *Matthew 4:19-20 (NKJV)*

> *He appointed twelve that they might be with him and that he might send them out to preach.*
> — *Mark 3:14 (NIV)*

2. He authorised and empowered His disciples to imitate Him and participate alongside Him in administering the Kingdom of God in their everyday lives.

   When Jesus had called the Twelve together, he gave them power and authority to drive out all demons and to cure diseases, and he sent them out to proclaim the kingdom of God and to heal the sick.

   — Luke 9:1-2 (NIV)

3. He stayed close and available to instruct them when they needed His help.

   Then the disciples came to Jesus in private and asked, "Why couldn't we drive it out?" He replied, "Because you have so little faith. Truly I tell you, if you have faith as small as a mustard seed, you can say to this mountain, 'Move from here to there,' and it will move. Nothing will be impossible for you."

   — Matthew 17:19-20 (NIV)

4. As the time came for Him to leave them and return to His Father's side, He stepped back, diminished His input, encouraged His disciples and prepared them to do the work on His behalf.

   I tell you the truth, anyone who believes in me will do the same works I have done, and even greater works, because I am going to be with the Father.

   — John 14:12 (NLT)

Jesus influenced His disciples by doing everyday life alongside them. As they walked together, they picked up His beliefs, His values, His thinking, His skills and everything in between! Understanding the limitation of His time on Earth, Jesus intentionally imparted everything that was in Him into those who followed Him, replicating Himself so that His work could continue on after His time had come to an end.

Jesus intentionally imparted everything that was in Him into those who followed Him, replicating Himself so that His work could continue on after His time had come to an end.

Sometimes, we can get put off by the failures of those we are leading or even intimidated by their success. The insecurity that accompanies wrong thinking can cause us to withhold ourselves in the fear that others will surpass us if we teach them everything we know. But Jesus shows us that true leaders and kings operate differently. He was not hesitant to declare that His followers would "do even greater things than these" (John 4:12). When you think like a king, you are committed to the success of those you lead and celebrate when they surpass your own achievements.

It seems so simple when you look at legacy in light of Jesus' example, but many find these steps very difficult to achieve, particularly when it is time to relinquish control and trust to those whom we are raising up to complete the work. Stepping back and diminishing as those you have invested into step up and increase is an essential yet painful step in the process of building a lasting legacy. Some never come to terms with this and hold on tightly to their position, forcing those who are coming behind them to search for opportunity and the space to grow elsewhere. All too often, I have witnessed highly successful marketplace leaders near the end of their career (or life), only to discover that there is no one left around them to carry their legacy forward. All of their successes and achievements suddenly seem insignificant in the absence of successors.

The Circle of Life

I love to use the illustration of the 'Circle of Life' to reiterate the constant change and transitions that we must embrace along the journey of life, in order to steward our God-given gifts and talents well.

We all start out in life as infants—completely useless, totally helpless and very inconvenient. All we do is eat, sleep and excrete. We are totally dependent on our parents and do nothing to contribute. We soon grow into toddlers and at this stage of life, it's all about 'me'—MY needs, MY comfort and MY feelings. We are entirely self-focussed and react badly when we are denied what we want. Our favourite word is 'mine' and we are introduced to the unpleasant concept of sharing for the first time.

From here, we move on to our teenage years where life is all about learning to manage our hormones. Boy meets girl and suddenly cares about what he is wearing and how he smells. As parents, we watch on in awe at the transformations that take place—not all of which are good—and we hope and pray that we have done enough in our child's impressionable years to set them up for their future. Our children remain incredibly self-focussed in this season.

As we mature into young adults and find our life partners, our world transitions from 'me' to 'us'. We begin to consider the needs and feelings of the one we are connected to, thinking less about ourselves and more about the other person. We willingly release our resources to the other, spending our time and money on the object of our affection.

I remember when this happened to me as a young man. Like most men, I had absolutely no interest in sunsets and kittens, yet the longer the relationship developed with my then girlfriend and now wife, Leonie, the more her interests became mine. I began noticing things I had never noticed before. I found myself marvelling at scenic views and wanting to share those moments with her. Things I had never cared about before suddenly became part of my consciousness because we were heading towards the 'oneness' of marriage.

It's true that loving relationships have a way of taking our focus off our indivdual selves, but even then, we still tend to be self-focussed as a couple—dreaming of travel, careers, houses and money.

From this point, we start raising families of our own. This is one of the most significant transitions in the 'circle of life'; that moment when you hold your newborn child in your arms and realise that your life will never be the same again. Immediately, the focus moves beyond 'me' and 'us' to the little helpless, tiny person we brought into the world—usually for selfish reasons. Our lives become all about THEM and we sacrifice our needs and desires in order to fulfil theirs.

Our natural legacy begins.

Though mostly a joyful and rewarding stage, raising children is challenging and demands death to self on so many levels. But it is certainly worth it, especially when they grow up and have children of their own. It is hard to top the joy of generations coming together to share life and celebrate special moments.

I have very fond memories of Christmases gone by. I remember my parents and grandparents sitting back and watching us kids tear open our gifts and scream with delight. They didn't want gifts themselves. They had everything they needed. Their joy was in watching the next generation experience the rewards of their labour. Simply put, they had mastered the art of diminishing in order to make space for the next generation to experience 'life to the full' and take their place in the spotlight. Even more amazing is the fact that they were able to see something of themselves reflected in the nature and appearance of those that they had invested their time, energy, love, wisdom and resources into over a lifetime.

This same powerful process of transitioning from selfishness to dying to self and finally living for others is as applicable to our work context as it is to our families. The greatest emotional and spiritual rewards await us when we invest intentionally into those who follow behind us. This is the essence of true and lasting legacy—exponential multiplication of blessing and wisdom that transcends generations and remains alive well after we have passed.

A Caretaker and Conduit

The Bible indicates that the first thirty years of Jesus' life were spent in relative obscurity, during which He increased in "wisdom, stature and favour with God and man" (Luke 2:52). But for the remaining three years of His life, Jesus poured Himself into others. He understood that His life was a conduit through which others could receive all that they needed to live a successful life themselves. He also knew that He had been given just one human lifetime to steward and care for others. As such, He drew out of it all that was needed to create a legacy of faith that would continue to influence the world thousands of years later. He did not seek to acquire wealth or status for Himself but instead, spent His energy on empowering others to fulfil their God-given destiny. When He finally returned to His Father, He left far more than a material inheritance for His 'family'. He left wisdom, faith, hope, values, security, confidence, boldness, trust, joy, peace, power, authority... the list goes on and on. These are the real treasures—the *gold* that remained after enduring the challenges and tribulations of His life on Earth, and we are all still benefiting from this powerful legacy today!

Will something of you be deposited in and seen in the lives of those who follow you after you are gone?

The truth is that God placed us on Earth to be caretakers of His creation. It was never ours to own, but simply to care for and pass down to future generations.

During the COVID19 pandemic, I found myself with more downtime than usual and enjoyed binging on Netflix. One series that really impacted my wife and I was *The Crown*—a story depicting the reign of Queen Elizabeth II, the current Queen of England. I am unsure how much 'poetic license' was given to the storyline, but all in all, it was based on the true story of the English royal family.

I remember one scene early on in the series, where the then King of England discovered that he was terminally ill and only had a short time to live. Despite his position as king, he was powerless over the disease and his imminent death.

Resigned to his fate, his focus suddenly shifted from his own reign to that of his daughter Elizabeth who was next in line to the throne. We watched as he gently drew her closer to himself with the purpose of fast-tracking her preparation so that she would be ready to rule when her time came.

On one occasion, he sent her on a tour of Australia in his place, despite the reservations of his advisors who considered her too young and inexperienced to represent him well. Unaware of her father's sickness, the queen-in-waiting did her best and at times blundered her way through the endless public engagements that awaited her. When she returned, he sat her down, discussed her experiences and instructed her with the wisdom he had acquired over his lifetime.

Prior to the King's diagnosis, Elizabeth enjoyed a childhood of privilege, free of the burden of rulership. However, with a new sense of urgency, her father began to include her in his daily routine, systematically teaching her how to deal with the responsibilities that came with the crown, and explaining the 'why' behind the 'what' of royal duty. Had he not intentionally taken the time to engage with his daughter at a new level of relationship, and impart as much of his wisdom into her life as he could, she would never have been prepared to take the throne. Instead, despite her grief at his death, she ascended the throne with confidence and security knowing that her father had prepared her well and believed in her ability to be a great queen. The king left this world knowing that a part of him would live on through her and that the throne would be secure for many generations to come.

What stood out to me the most was his INTENTIONALITY. The greatest gift he could leave his daughter was not extreme wealth, but *preparedness* and *confidence* in her ability to succeed and take her place of influence in the history books. While she would go on to write her own story, she was able to stand upon his shoulders, draw from what had been imparted into her and carry his values in her heart. Now in her nineties, I am sure that she intends to leave the same gift of preparedness to her own children and grandchildren.

As kings called to marketplace ministry, I hope that you catch this important message of legacy as we conclude our journey together. Born into privilege and assured a throne of authority and dominion, true kings understand that they are caretakers of a legacy that began generations before their time in history and will continue long after their journey is over—if they steward the gift they have been given well. They are conduits of blessing. Their lives are not their own, but belong to those over whom they have been called to rule and serve.

Sound familiar?

Jesus was the perfect example of a servant king. Not caught up with His own greatness and power, but secure in the love of His Father and confident in His divine calling, He remained focussed on the ones He was called to serve. He knew He would be provided for and protected by His Father until He had fulfilled His purpose. His job was to impart something of Himself into the lives of those who would continue to run with the same purpose long after His own time on Earth had come to an end. This brought Him the joy and satisfaction that only a life poured out for others can bring. While His primary calling was to die on the cross and purchase the salvation of humanity, He also invested His life into preparing and equipping others to represent Him and to continue spreading His message of salvation for generations to come. Likewise, walking in our personal destiny must go hand in hand with imparting into and preparing others to carry our legacy (and God's) into the future. The two are inseparable and equally important.

Empowered by the Holy Spirit, Jesus could have facilitated the salvation of the world single-handedly, yet chose to partner with human beings. This is the incredible mystery of being a Christian. Sometimes we forget the huge privilege that we have been given to partner with God to see His Kingdom established on Earth as it is in Heaven....not OUR kingdom but HIS Kingdom. Just like Elizabeth's father, the King of England, our Heavenly Father intentionally takes us through life's circumstances, strategically preparing us to rule and reign in the marketplace when our time comes. While we might be enjoying the spoils of privilege, we must never forget our responsibility to learn from our predecessors, rule with integrity and impart our knowledge into the upcoming generation. This is the 'circle of life' as God intended.

I have found that my role in this season is that of a coach and mentor to the next generation of emerging leaders. The greatest treasures that I hold are experience, wisdom and insight. The gift that I can give is my time as I position myself to be poured out into others. I can honestly say that the fulfilment I feel in this role exceeds any thrill that I have ever

What I have been through in my life was not without purpose, but intended by God to enable me to create pathways for others felt in pursuit of my own significance and conquests. It is the knowledge that what I have been through, endured and overcome in my life was not without purpose, but was intended by God to enable me to create pathways for others and to bring hope, security and comfort for their journey.

It's said that Charles Spurgeon implored people to "carve your name on hearts, not on marble". What wise words!

So, to each one of you who feel called to marketplace ministry, I urge you to push beyond the limitations of self-focussed exploits and the accumulation of personal wealth. There is even greater purpose for your life. These natural spoils of our hard work bring some temporary satisfaction for sure, but they will never satisfy our desire to leave a significant and lasting imprint on the Earth. This can only be achieved by tapping into our God-given purpose and building a legacy that reaches beyond our lifetime and into eternity.

> *Do not store up for yourselves treasures on earth, where moths and vermin destroy, and where thieves break in and steal. But store up for yourselves treasures in heaven, where moths and vermin do not destroy, and where thieves do not break in and steal. For where your treasure is, there your heart will be also.*
> *— Matthew 6:19-21 (NIV)*

If we are truly going to be the light of the world and bring our influence to bear in seeing cities transformed, we must be open to examine and change our behaviours. We must surround ourselves with godly people and renewed practices that reposition us to achieve our God-given purpose.

So where do we start?

It all begins with renewed thinking.

Even if you forget some of its contents over time, I hope that this book has left an indelible imprint in your heart borne from moments of encounter and impartation. I hope it has not merely changed some of your beliefs, but has helped you wholly embrace the Kingdom-thinking that aligns with the King of kings Himself—Jesus.

SCAN & WATCH

This is your moment. Will you put it all on the line and rise up?

It's time to think like a king.

NOTES

Chapter 1: Winning Cities

Page 20:   "I remember that view very vividly": Rhianna King, "The Moment Perth Became the City of Lights", *WA Today*, 17/02/2012, https://www.watoday.com.au/national/western-australia/the-moment-perth-became-the-city-of-lights-20120217-1te0z.html

Page 22:   "render as excellent": Note also Bauer and Danker's definition [BDAG, 3rd. ed., p. 258] "to influence one's opinion about another so as to enhance the latter's reputation, praise, honor, extol"

Chapter 2: Be

Page 29:   "You can live in this world": T. D. Jakes, *Identity*, (e-book: Destiny Image Publishers, 2015), 9.

Chapter 3: Think

Page 58:   "278 times the average wage": https://www.cnbc.com/2019/08/16/ ceos-see-pay-grow-1000percent-and-now-make-278-times-the-average-worker.html

Chapter 6: The Power of Focus

Page 126:   "When you become successful": Craig Groeschel hosted an interview Michael Hyatt entitled "Vision for the Future", https://www.life.church/leadershippodcast/q-a-with-michael-hyatt-vision-for-the-future/

Chapter 8: Building a Winning Team

Page 159: "No organization can depend on genius": Peter Drucker, *Management: Tasks, Responsibilities, Practices*, (New York: Harper Business, 1973), 455.

Page 178: "over a thousand people": In 1992, six years after Microsoft shares were offered to the public with generous stock options for employees, approximately 2,200 Microsoft employees were found to be millionaires. https://www.nytimes.com/1992/06/28/business/microsoft-s-unlikely-millionaires.html

Chapter 9: Shift

Page 193: "Michael Gerber's book": Michael Gerber, *E-Myth Mastery: The Seven Essential Disciplines for Building a World Class Company* (e-Book: HarperCollins e-books, 2009).

Page 193: "Knowing how to do the work": Michael Gerber, *E-Myth Mastery: The Seven Essential Disciplines for Building a World Class Company* (e-Book: HarperCollins e-books, 2009), 36.

Page 196: "The entrepreneur builds an enterprise": Michael Gerber, *E-Myth Mastery: The Seven Essential Disciplines for Building a World Class Company* (e-Book: HarperCollins e-books, 2009), 36.

Page 206: "Saving people money": https://corporate.walmart.com/our-story/our-history

Page 206: "The combined wealth of Sam's descendents": https://www.businessinsider.com/how-the-waltons-spend-their-fortune-2017-7?r=AU&IR=T